# GREAT TASTING NATURAL FOOD
# discover organic

First published in Great Britain in 2011 by
Sustain: the alliance for better food and farming
94 White Lion St, London N1 9PF

Compiled and edited by Sam Carter
Photography by Richard Faulks
Design by Mik Baines

ISBN 978-1-903060-50-6

A CIP catalogue record for this book is available from the British Library.

Printed and bound in Great Britain by RAP Spiderweb Ltd

# CONTENTS

OUR ORGANIC LOVERS ARE A PASSIONATE BUNCH. TURN TO THEIR PAGES FOR SOME TRULY INSPIRED RECIPES, THEN DISCOVER OUR COLLECTION OF MOUTH-WATERING SEASONAL MEALS... ENJOY!

> "ORGANIC FOOD IS FOR EVERYONE, AND FOR EVERY DAY OF THE WEEK"

# WELCOME!

## WITH THE EXPLOSION OF INTEREST IN OUR FOOD AND WHERE IT COMES FROM AS WELL AS GROWING CONCERN FOR THE ENVIRONMENT, WE KNOW THAT ORGANIC IS HERE TO STAY.

What we eat and what we feed our families is one of the most fundamental choices we can make. We all have our own reasons for choosing organic food, and for me I'm passionate about feeding my young family with the most natural, great tasting food. For others it may be that it's good for animal welfare or better for nature.

We at the Why I Love Organic campaign want to share that passion, and what better way than to present a selection of mouthwatering recipes that showcase organic ingredients at their very best. Some people you'll certainly recognise are on board to share their secrets: Kate Humble, David Haye, Raymond Blanc and Jody Scheckter, among others – all of them are here with their personal tips and stories.

There's plenty of practical advice to help you in the kitchen too, and to let you know a little of the inspiring story of organic food. And in leafing through the personal tales and favourite meals, a strong message emerges. Organic food is for everyone, and for every day of the week. These recipes are so accessible, and the organic ingredients so simple to find, that we hope you'll come on board and Discover Organic.

Catherine Fookes
WHY I LOVE ORGANIC

# WHY I LOVE ORGANIC

> ❝
>
> ### SARA COX
> RADIO DJ
>
> WITH THREE YOUNG CHILDREN, IT'S IMPORTANT THAT I'M GIVING THEM THE BEST TO EAT. THROUGH BUYING ORGANIC I CAN REST ASSURED THAT THE FOOD THEY ARE EATING IS NATURAL AND GOOD FOR THEM ❞

> ❝
>
> ### PIP FAULKS
> SUPPORTER
>
> THE MORE PEOPLE LOVE AND DEMAND ORGANIC FOOD THE BETTER IT IS NOT ONLY FOR US, BUT ON A WIDER SCALE IT HAS A HUGE KNOCK-ON EFFECT FOR OUR ENTIRE ECO-SYSTEM. IF THERE WERE MORE ORGANIC CROPS, MY BEES WOULD MAKE MORE ORGANIC HONEY WHICH IN TURN I WOULD LOVE ❞

> ❝
>
> ### MUAN
> SUPPORTER
>
> I BUY EVERY POSSIBLE THING ORGANIC BECAUSE I CARE DEEPLY ABOUT WHAT IMPACT THE THINGS I BUY AND USE HAVE ON THE ENVIRONMENT ❞

> ❝
>
> ### ZAC GOLDSMITH
> MP
>
> AT A TIME WHEN IT'S ALMOST IMPOSSIBLE TO KNOW IF THE FOOD WE ARE EATING HAS BEEN PRODUCED CLEANLY AND ETHICALLY, THE ONE STANDARD WE CAN ALL TRUST IS ORGANIC. THAT'S WHY I ABSOLUTELY BACK THE 'WHY I LOVE ORGANIC' CAMPAIGN AND WISH IT ALL THE SUCCESS IN THE WORLD ❞

> ❝
>
> ### BOB FLOWERDEW
> PRESENTER
>
> I LOVE ORGANIC FOOD, ESPECIALLY WHEN IT'S MY OWN HOME-GROWN PRODUCE, SIMPLY BECAUSE IT TASTES SO GOOD! ❞

> ❝
>
> ### EMMA
> SUPPORTER
>
> WE GARDEN ORGANICALLY (INCLUDING OUR VEG AND SOON-TO-ARRIVE CHICKENS), TRY TO BUY ORGANIC FOOD WHERE POSSIBLE AND USE MAINLY ORGANIC SKINCARE AND COTTON WHERE POSSIBLE. SINCE WE HAD KIDS WE HAVE BEEN FAR MORE AWARE OF IT ❞

# OUR ROOTS!

UNTIL THE DAWN OF THE TWENTIETH CENTURY, ALL FOOD IS ORGANIC – THERE IS NO OTHER WAY! BUT THEN COMES THE INVENTION AND INCREASING USE OF SYNTHETIC NITROGEN FERTILIZERS AND PESTICIDES. SOME FARMS RESIST THESE DEVELOPMENTS – THE ORIGINAL ORGANIC PIONEERS. SO, **HOW DID WE GET TO WHERE WE ARE TODAY?**

## 1924

In Germany, Rudolf Steiner's **Spiritual Foundations for the Renewal of Agriculture**, published in 1924, leads to the popularisation of biodynamic agriculture, probably the first comprehensive organic farming system and based on Steiner's spiritual and philosophical teachings.

## 1939-45

Britain stands alone in the Second World War and the '**Dig For Victory**' campaign is launched in an effort to prevent the nation from being starved into submission. By necessity, organic methods are used.

## 1967

The first **organic standards** are established.

The first use of the term 'organic farming' is by Lord Northbourne, set out in his book, **Look to the Land** (1940) in which he describes a holistic, ecologically balanced approach to farming. Lord Northbourne was the first to draw a comparison between 'chemical farming' and 'organic farming'.

## 1940

Lady Balfour's landmark book **The Living Soil** is published – an inspiring vision of the organic movement which leads to the establishment of the Soil Association.

## 1946

Craig Sams and his brother Gregory open **Seed**, the first organic macrobiotic restaurant in London's Notting Hill. At the time, such an approach was rare, and potential investors questioned whether this 'fad' was going to last. Undeterred, Sams set up the brands **Whole Earth** and, with his wife Josephine Fairley, **Green & Black's**.

## 1960s

Organic certification is introduced, and the organic logo and organic food labelling standards follow closely behind.

## 1973

## 1990s

Organic baby food flies off shelves. In 1992, Lizzie Vann sets up baby food pioneers, **Organix**, and a new generation of children begin to eat organic food.

## 978

The pesticide DDT is banned across Europe from most agricultural use, with a total ban in 1983.

## 1993

Organic sales top **£100 million**.

## 2005

Organic sales reach **£2 billion**, and Tesco carries 1,200 lines of organic food.

**Waitrose** is the first supermarket to stock organic products.

## 1983

## 1983

Organic standards ban animal protein from organic livestock feed for cattle and sheep, rightly predicting serious consequences. Three years after the ban, the first case of **BSE** (mad cow disease) is confirmed.

## 1988

Animal protein is banned from all ruminant feed.

**THE NOUGHTIES**
A FOOD REVOLUTION SWEEPS THE COUNTRY. GROWING YOUR OWN AND KNOWING ABOUT LOCAL, SEASONAL AND ORGANIC FOOD HAS NEVER BEEN MORE POPULAR

# KATE HUMBLE
## TV PRESENTER

**I BUY ORGANIC BECAUSE OF THE WILDLIFE FACTOR. I AM 100% IN FAVOUR OF FARMERS LOOKING AFTER WILDLIFE AND MANY FARMERS DO THAT. BUT WITH ORGANIC YOU GET THE EXTRA REASSURANCE ON THE LABEL**

Making the most of the land available to you (even if it's just a patch the size of a postage stamp) to grow your own food is just such a fantastic and worthwhile thing to do – there's nothing like pulling a carrot out of the ground, wiping it on your jeans and eating it right there and then. I was fortunate to grow up in the countryside – picking tomatoes with my grandfather and podding peas with my grandmother – but it's never too late to learn, and growing your own food is easier than you might think (honest!). Before you know it, you'll have more fresh food than you know what to do with. But if that happens, simply trade some of it with something your neighbour has produced! I swap my chickens for my neighbour's beef, and I love how food provides the perfect excuse to go and see people.

I buy organic because of the wildlife factor. I am 100% in favour of farmers looking after wildlife and many farmers do that. But with organic you get the extra reassurance on the label. Decent meat reared by local farmers employing high animal welfare practices is really worth splashing out on. Take sausages, for example: at 90 per cent pork (and I'm talking about the proper meat), one is practically a meal in itself!

The British countryside is an amazing resource, but with a rising population, the demand for plentiful and cheap food is growing. This precious land is under a lot of pressure, so it's important that we give organic farmers and small producers our full support. By making the right food purchases, you can really make a difference, and even if you live in the city, you can still be a good guardian of the countryside.

Catalan chicken

Duck egg and asparagus

# CATALAN CHICKEN

I PRODUCE CHICKENS AT HOME AND ONE DAY
I TOOK ONE ROUND TO GIVE TO A FRIEND.
TOGETHER WE TRANSFORMED IT AND CREATED THIS
RECIPE: CATALAN CHICKEN! THE DISH COMBINES
CHOCOLATE, PRUNES, CINNAMON AND PINE NUTS,
WHICH ALL REGULARLY APPEAR ON CATALAN MENUS
IN ONE GUISE OR ANOTHER. IT MAY SOUND LIKE A
STRANGE COMBINATION, BUT IT IS DELICIOUS!

**Method**

Soften the onion in the oil very slowly, with the lid on for as long as it takes. At least 15 minutes.

Whizz up the tin of tomatoes and, when the onions are soft and translucent, add the tomatoes and crushed garlic. Cook for another 10–15 minutes gently simmering so it reduces. This is the basis of lots of Catalan dishes, and is called the sofregit.

Brown the chicken and add to the tomatoes and onions. Add the rest of the ingredients bar the chocolate and pine nuts. Season generously. Put the lid on the pan and bring to a simmer on a low heat. Meanwhile toast the pine nuts and put aside.

After 30 minutes or so, when the chicken is cooked, grate the chocolate into the pan, and add the toasted pine nuts.

Serve with boiled new potatoes with parsley and a salad.

**Ingredients**

1 tbsp olive oil
1 onion, finely chopped
1 organic free-range chicken, cut into at least 8 pieces
1 tin of tomatoes
1 small bag of prunes
4 cloves of garlic, crushed
A couple of handfuls of pine nuts
1 tbsp ground almonds
1 tsp cinnamon
25g dark organic cooking chocolate

# DUCK EGG
# AND ASPARAGUS

THE VERY DEFINITION OF SIMPLICITY, BUT WITH
ENGLISH ASPARAGUS IN SEASON AND A FRESH AND
PERFECTLY BOILED DUCK EGG, DIFFICULT TO BEAT

**Method**

Bend the asparagus spears to break off the woody lower part.
Trim with a sharp knife. Steam gently until tender all the way
through.

Meanwhile, boil the duck egg for 3 to 4 minutes, so that the
yolk is still runny. Slice the top off the egg, add a dot of butter
and season.

Then dip the asparagus into the yolk, just like you do with
toast soldiers, and enjoy the heavenly combination.

**Ingredients**

A few fresh organic
asparagus spears
1 organic free-range
duck egg
Knob of butter
Salt and black pepper

"IT'S NEVER TOO LATE TO LEARN, AND GROWING
YOUR OWN FOOD IS EASIER THAN YOU MIGHT
THINK (HONEST!)"

# DAVID HAYE
BOXER AND FORMER-HEAVYWEIGHT
CHAMPION OF THE WORLD
I LOVE TO EAT THIS REFRESHING
TROPICAL ORGANIC SALAD AS A
STARTER DISH. IT'S NICE AND LIGHT
AND SIMPLY PACKED WITH ENZYMES

# RAW SALAD

**Method**

Peel the papaya.

Lop the spiky head off the pineapple and slice off the base, then stand the pineapple up and run a long knife around the edges of the flesh, making sure you cut all the way to the bottom. Then simply lift off the skin so you're left with a log of flesh.

Coarsely shred or chop the fruit and mix together. Sprinkle over pumpkin seeds.

To make the vinaigrette, whisk the lemon juice and vinegar into the hemp seed oil until you have an emulsion. Season to taste.

Dress the salad, mixing well with your hands, and eat immediately.

**Ingredients**

For the salad:
1 organic papaya
1 organic pineapple
2 tbsp pumpkin seeds

For the vinaigrette:
1 tsp lemon juice
1 tsp coconut vinegar
3 tbsp hemp seed oil
Himalayan rock salt

JEAN CAZALS

# RAYMOND BLANC
## CHEF

I LOVE ORGANIC FOOD BECAUSE I KNOW THAT THE FOOD ON MY PLATE HAS COME FROM A FARMER WHO PRACTISES HEALTHY AND SUSTAINABLE AGRICULTURE. SUCH A FARMER WILL BE SOMEONE WHO SHARES MY OWN ETHICAL VALUES AND HELPS ME RECONNECT WITH MY OWN FOOD CULTURE AND TRADITIONS

# APPLE TART 'MAMAN BLANC'

IN MY BOOK, MAMAN BLANC MAKES THE BEST APPLE TART, AND THE SECRET OF THIS DISH IS CHOOSING THE RIGHT APPLES. FOR AN EQUALLY DELICIOUS FRUIT TART, SIMPLY SUBSTITUTE THE APPLES FOR PLUMS, APRICOTS OR CHERRIES, AND FOLLOW THE SAME RECIPE

## Method
To make the pastry, use a food processor to pulse together the flour, butter and salt until you reach a sandy texture. Add the egg and water, and pulse again.

Transfer the dough onto a lightly floured work surface and knead with the palms of your hands for 30 seconds, or until the dough is smooth and well combined. Continues over

## Ingredients
Serves 6

For the pastry dough:
250g plain flour
Pinch of sea salt
125g unsalted butter, diced, at room temperature
1 medium free-range egg
1 tsp cold water

For the filling:
15g unsalted butter
Half tbsp lemon juice
65g caster sugar
Half tbsp Calvados (optional)
3–4 organic Cox's Orange Pippin, Worcester, Russet or Braeburn apples, peeled, cored and cut into 10 segments per apple
100ml double cream
1 medium free-range egg
1–2 tbsp icing sugar, for dusting

19

# APPLE TART
# 'MAMAN BLANC' CONTINUED

With the palm of your hand flatten the dough to 1cm thick, then sandwich it between two large sheets of clingfilm. Chill in the fridge for 30 minutes.

Preheat the oven to 220°C, Gas mark 7. Place a baking tray into the oven to preheat.

Roll out the chilled dough, still sandwiched in clingfilm, to a 2mm thickness.

Place a 22cm diameter, 2cm deep tart ring on a baking tray lined with greaseproof paper. Remove the top layer of clingfilm then carefully turn the dough over and drape it into the tart ring with the second layer of clingfilm facing up. Press the dough fully into the ring then discard the clingfilm. Trim off any excess dough.

Press and pinch with your fingers to raise the height of the dough edges to 2mm above the tart ring. With a fork, prick the bottom of the tart. Chill in the fridge for 20 minutes.

Meanwhile, make the filling by heating the butter, lemon juice and 15g of the sugar in a small saucepan until the butter has melted and the sugar has dissolved. Remove from the heat and stir in the Calvados. Set aside.

When the tart case has chilled, arrange the apple segments in concentric circles, overlapping the slices as you go then brush the apples all over with the Calvados mixture.

Slide the tart ring onto the preheated baking tray and bake for 10 minutes.

Reduce the oven temperature to 200°C, Gas mark 6, then continue to cook for a further 20 minutes, until the pastry is pale golden brown and the apples have caramelised.

Whisk together the double cream, egg and the remaining 50g caster sugar. Pour into the tart and bake for a further 10 minutes until the cream mixture has just set.

To serve, remove the tart from the oven and set aside for 1 hour to cool slightly, then carefully remove the tart ring. Dust with icing sugar and serve immediately.

From *Kitchen Secrets* by Raymond Blanc.

# LORRAINE PASCALE
## FORMER MODEL AND TV CHEF

MY FAVOURITE ORGANIC MOMENT IS WHEN WE HAVE A ROAST CHICKEN. I SMOTHER IT WITH BUTTER, STUFF IT WITH TARRAGON AND GARLIC AND COOK IT UNTIL IT IS CRISP. SITTING DOWN WITH THE FAMILY AND EATING IT TOGETHER IS THE HIGHLIGHT OF MY WEEK. I LIKE TO USE ORGANIC WHEN I CAN AS I FEEL ORGANIC HAS MORE FLAVOUR AND IT IS GREAT TO KNOW IT HAS FEWER PESTICIDES

# ROSEMARY AND SEA SALT FOCCACIA BREAD

THIS DELICIOUS BREAD IS GREAT FOR SHARING, AND TASTES EVEN BETTER WHEN YOU USE REALLY FINE EXTRA VIRGIN OLIVE OIL. I HIDE MY GOOD BOTTLE OF EXTRA VIRGIN ON THE TOP SHELF OF A CUPBOARD, AWAY FROM PRYING HANDS – IT'S FAR TOO NICE TO BE USED FOR UNWORTHY COOKING TASKS LIKE FRYING EGGS. BUT FOR MAKING FOCCACIA, IT'S WELL WORTH USING, AND THE IMPERIAL BOTTLE OF OIL MAKES A RARE APPEARANCE

### Ingredients

Makes 1 large flat loaf
500g organic strong white bread flour, plus extra for dusting
2 tsp salt
1 x 7g sachet of fast action dried yeast
80ml olive oil, plus extra for drizzling
150–250ml warm water
Vegetable oil or oil spray, for oiling
1 bunch of fresh rosemary
Large pinch of sea salt

**Method**
Dust a large flat baking tray with flour.

Put the flour in a large bowl, add the salt and yeast, then add the olive oil plus enough warm water to make a dough that is soft but not sticky. Continues over

The more water that can be added (the full 250ml is great) then the lighter the bread will be. But it can take some perseverance. Even if the dough feels sloppy at first, resist the temptation to add more flour as it will make the dough too heavy.

Knead the dough for about 10 minutes by hand on a lightly floured work surface or for 5 minutes if using an electric mixer fitted with a dough hook. The dough should feel stretchy when pulled.

To test if it is ready, make a ball with the dough then, using a well-floured finger, prod a shallow indent in the side. If the dough springs back and the indent disappears, it is ready to shape.

Shape the dough into an oval and place it on the prepared baking tray. Flatten it out to about 30cm long and 20cm wide. Cover the dough with oiled clingfilm, making sure it is airtight.

Preheat the oven to 200°C, Gas mark 6. Leave the dough in a warm place for about 1 hour, or until it has almost doubled in size.

With a floured index finger press holes in the dough at regular intervals, about 4cm apart in rows across the dough, pressing right down to the bottom. Take 3cm long sprigs of the rosemary and push them into the holes.

Sprinkle some sea salt over the dough and place it in the top third of the oven. Bake for about 25–30 minutes or until the bread is well risen, light golden brown and sounds hollow when tapped underneath.

Remove from the oven, drizzle with the remaining olive oil and leave to cool on the baking tray.

This is perfect served warm as a starter or indeed as a meal in itself with fresh tomatoes, artichokes and cold meats, or with a steaming bowl of hot soup.

" I HIDE MY GOOD BOTTLE OF EXTRA VIRGIN ON THE TOP SHELF OF A CUPBOARD, AWAY FROM PRYING HANDS "

# ANTHEA TURNER
## TV PERSONALITY

I LOVE VEGETABLES – ALL OF THEM! I CANNOT EVEN NAME A SINGLE VEGETABLE I DON'T LIKE. IN AN IDEAL WORLD, IF I HAD MORE TIME, I'D GROW MY OWN. UNFORTUNATELY, I JUST SPEND TOO MUCH TIME AWAY FROM HOME AND IT CAN'T BE DONE. FORTUNATELY I'VE GOT SOME GREAT LOCAL SHOPS SUPPLYING ORGANIC PRODUCE – THEY'RE MY 'VEGETABLE PATCH'

# FRUITS OF THE EARTH MEDLEY

ONE OF MY FAVOURITE WAYS OF COOKING AND PRESENTING ALL THE WONDERFUL VEG, SHOWING OFF THEIR RICH COLOURS AND SUCCULENT TASTES, IS WITH A ROASTED MEDLEY OF ROOTS. I SERVE THIS WITH ROAST PORK AND ROASTED POTATOES. FOR A SUNDAY LUNCH I FINISH OFF WITH APPLE CRUMBLE AND ICE CREAM – HOME MADE IF I HAVE THE TIME. EVERYONE IS HAPPY

**Method**

Pre-heat the oven to 200°C, Gas mark 6.

Wash, trim and peel the root veg. Cut all the roots into generous chunks.

Peel and quarter the red onion, bash the garlic cloves (but leave the skin on) and finely chop the herbs.

Put all the vegetables in a large bowl, add the oil, bay leaves and chopped herbs, and mix really well. Season liberally.

Tip all into a sturdy, large roasting tray and put in the pre-heated oven for around 40 minutes, turning occasionally.

**Ingredients**

Serves 8 as a side dish

A selection of organic root veg, preferably in season.
I'd recommend a mixture of parsnip, butternut squash, carrots, baby turnips and sweet potato, total around 1kg.
1 red onion (large)
6 garlic cloves
4 bay leaves
2 sprigs of thyme
2 sprigs of rosemary
4 tbsp olive oil
Salt and pepper

# MATT TEBBUTT
## CHEF AND TV PRESENTER

**WHEN MY WIFE AND I FLED LONDON TEN YEARS AGO AND SET UP OUR RESTAURANT, THE FOXHUNTER, IN THE IDYLLIC WELSH COUNTRYSIDE, IT SEEMED SO OBVIOUS AND NATURAL TO BUY LOCALLY AND ORGANICALLY GROWN FOOD, IN SEASON**

Old Spot cooked in milk and cinnamon

Braised topside of beef

Leg of mutton

Sautéed eel with mustard, cider & cream

Elderflower fritters with lime

"I woke up to the importance of buying seasonal produce while still in London: I'd never really been much of a fruit person until one day I was handed this amazing peach, picked at its best at the height of the season. The fruit's colour, flavour and texture were just unbelievable – miles away from the sad-looking fellas you see in the supermarkets in December. Since that peach, I've never looked back, and now I base my restaurant menu entirely on what's in season (and that means whatever's hanging around in the hedgerows, too!).

I can really tell the difference between organic and non-organic fruit, vegetables and herbs. Coriander or basil that hasn't been messed around with is just so much more intense than the mass-produced stuff. And organic rocket will practically blow your head off! Have a taste, and you'll realise why it goes so well with mild and creamy Parmesan cheese. Organic mushrooms also wipe the floor with their non-organic counterparts – the organic ones are much bigger, smellier and tastier.

For a real sense of why organic food matters, go for a walk in the countryside on a fine summer's day. Just seeing a vibrant natural meadow, filled with a dizzying number of grasses, flowers and happy insects, reminds me what the British countryside should look like – unspoilt and gently worked."

# OLD SPOT COOKED IN MILK, CINNAMON, BAY AND LEMON

**Method**

Season the pork all over and seal in a hot tray big enough to hold the pork as a whole. Add the butter, garlic and thyme, let the pork sizzle to extract the flavour.

Add the milk almost to cover, add the lemon zest and half of the juice, cinnamon sticks and bay leaves.

Put into a low (150°C, Gas mark 2) oven and cook uncovered for 1.5–2 hours.

Remove the pork. Keep warm and skim the sauce of excess fat, taste and reduce to sauce consistency. The sauce should be nicely curdled.

Cut the meat into slices and spoon over the sauce, soft onions and cinnamon sticks.

Serve with some boiled potatoes and seasonal veg.

**Ingredients**

1 whole loin of best quality organic Old Spot 3–4kg, boneless and skinless
30g fresh thyme
2 lemons pared and juiced
2ltrs of milk approx. (needs to be enough to cover pork)
100g unsalted butter
Olive oil
3 heads of garlic cut in half
20g cinnamon sticks
4-5 bay leaves
2 white onions cut into quarters and peeled
10g mixed peppercorns

# BRAISED TOPSIDE OF BEEF WITH ANCHOVY AND ONION

**Method**

Pre-heat the oven to 150°C, Gas mark 2.

Rub a casserole dish (with lid) all over inside with butter and scatter in some of the onions. Season the beef and layer over the onions.

Continue to layer beef, onions and seasoning. Smear the underside of a sheet of greaseproof paper with more butter and lay it over the top.

Put the lid on the pot and put over a flame until it starts to sizzle. Then place in the oven and leave for two hours or so until meat is very tender.

Place the rest of the ingredients in a food processor and blitz to make paste.

Stir the paste into the meat and the juices. Replace lid and leave to infuse for 30 minutes. Serve with mash, Jersey Royals or country bread.

**Ingredients**

1–2 kg organic topside cut into portion sized steaks
6 white onions cut thickly into half moons
2 pkts / 500g unsalted butter
Salt and pepper
A few bay leaves

2–3 garlic cloves crushed
1–2 tbsp red wine vinegar
6 tbsp olive oil
5–6 anchovy fillets chopped up
2 dried red chillies
1 very large handful flat leaf parsley

# LEG OF MUTTON
# WITH CAPER SAUCE

**Method**

Season the leg all over. Generously rub the inside of a casserole dish with the butter. Throw in the sliced onions and the aromatics (wrapped in some muslin) around the leg, tip in the wine and once again, season generously.

Butter a cartouche (greaseproof paper) and lay on top. Cover the pot with a heavy lid and roast for around 2 hours at 140°C, Gas mark 1.

Meanwhile, reduce the stock by half and set aside.

When the mutton has cooked, take off about 1 litre of the cooking stock and onions, pour onto the chicken stock. Reduce again by half. Add the capers and the double cream, then bring back to the boil and simmer for a few minutes.

Slice the mutton and spoon over the caper sauce. Serve with small boiled potatoes and vegetables of your choice.

**Ingredients**

1 leg of organic mutton
6 large onions, sliced
5 bay leaves
200g unsalted butter
3 star anise
1 stick of rosemary
1 tsp black peppercorns
500ml white wine

500ml double cream
1 ltr chicken stock
6 tbsp small capers
Salt and pepper

# SAUTÉED EEL WITH MUSTARD, CIDER AND CREAM

**Method**

Cut the eel through the bone into 1 inch chunks.

Lightly flour, season and colour in a pan with the thyme and garlic.

Add the cider, bay leaves and reduce by two-thirds.

Add the fish stock and simmer for 10 minutes.

Stir in the mustards, add the cream and bring to the boil.

Taste and season.

Re-heat the savoy cabbage in boiling water, then drain and serve.

Spoon the eel and mustard sauce over the top.

**Ingredients**

1 medium/large fresh eel (dead!)
1 bottle organic dry cider
1 sprig of thyme
1 clove of garlic
2 bay leaves
1 savoy cabbage, finely shredded and blanched
Wholegrain mustard
Dijon mustard
Double cream
Olive oil
50g unsalted butter
250ml fish stock

# ELDERFLOWER FRITTERS WITH YOGURT AND LIME

**Method**

Mix all the yogurt ingredients together and reserve.

Make up the batter and set aside.

Pick over the inside of the elderflower heads to remove any insects. Lightly flour and dip into the batter. Deep fry for 2–3 mins at 175°C until golden.

Sprinkle with caster sugar and serve immediately with the lime yogurt.

**Ingredients**

For the yogurt:
300ml organic Greek yogurt
1 tbsp icing sugar
1 lime juiced and zested
Half vanilla pod, de-seeded

To make up a batter:
450g fine flour
1 bottle of organic lager (330ml)
Enough sparkling water to make a slack paste (500ml)
25g fresh yeast

4 tbsp caster sugar
6–8 heads of elderflower on stalks

# JODY SCHECKTER
## FORMER RACING DRIVER AND FOUNDER OF LAVERSTOKE PARK FARM

IN A WAY, I DON'T LIKE TO USE THE WORD 'ORGANIC' – SOME PEOPLE THINK IT SMACKS OF ELITISM. BUT THAT'S ABSOLUTE RUBBISH: ORGANIC MEANS GREAT TASTING NATURAL FOOD AND THAT IS FOR EVERYBODY

I guess I've always had a passion for keeping animals and working the land – I first kept chickens when I was just 8 years old and used to love helping my parents grow vegetables in the garden. But a few years ago my wife gave me a book on organics, and the whole concept made so much sense to me that I read on and on. Now I've got 500 books on the subject, many of them from the beginning of the last century when everybody ate natural food – there just wasn't anything else!

But just because organic farming uses fewer artificial pesticides and additives, it doesn't mean it's stuck in the dark ages. I believe in using modern science to try to understand nature better, which is why I've got a whole team of scientists working on my organic farm.

Want to know the key to achieving the best-tasting and healthiest food? Biodiversity. Rather than feeding my farm animals the same old grain day in and day out, I let them graze on a 'mixed salad' of 31 different herbs, clovers and grasses. And I've planted 13 km of hedges and 130,000 trees on my farm (not including the vineyard!) to increase diversity.

You can definitely taste the difference between organic and non-organic food. If you don't believe me, just sample a scoop of my Laverstoke Park Farm Ice Cream: the proof, as they say, is in the pudding.

Organic black pudding

Ciliegine mozarella Treasure hunt salad

Bread and butter pudding

Organic game scotch eggs

Buffalo bolognaise

# ORGANIC BLACK PUDDING AND NITRATE-FREE BACON ON GRILLED SOURDOUGH, WITH A SOFT POACHED FREE-RANGE EGG AND HOLLANDAISE SAUCE

## Method

Fry the bacon in its own fat in a non-stick pan until it's as crispy as you like it. Then remove from the heat, set aside and keep warm.

Fry the black pudding slices in the bacon fat, keeping the heat at medium to allow the pudding to cook through without blackening too much on the surface. As black pudding is already cooked, you're just heating it through and melting the fat.

Heat a deep pan of water to just below boiling and drop in the white wine vinegar (adding more if your eggs are not that fresh).

Gently crack the egg and slowly lower the contents into the hot water. A fresh egg should hold together so there's no need to swirl the water. Cook the eggs without allowing the water to boil until when you hold them in a slotted spoon they are soft to the touch but not too wobbly.

While the eggs are poaching, brush your sourdough with a little olive oil and grill the slices on a griddle pan, turning them once to achieve some nice sear lines. Then set aside your bacon, black pudding and toast in a warm oven for a minute or so as you prepare your Hollandaise sauce.

To make the sauce, place the egg yolks, lemon juice, mustard and Tabasco in a blending jug.

Melt the butter in a pan until it boils, but do not allow it to brown. As the butter reaches the boil, turn on the blender. While the eggs are blending, pour the boiling butter in a steady stream into the egg mixture. The heat of the butter will cook the eggs almost instantly and the sauce will thicken.

Now assemble your breakfast!

## Ingredients

Per person
1cm-thick slice of organic black pudding
2 rashers of nitrate-free smoked streaky bacon
1 tbsp white wine vinegar
1 fresh free-range egg
1 thick slice of good-quality sourdough bread
A little olive oil

For enough Hollandaise sauce to feed 4 hungry breakfasters (adjust quantities accordingly):
3 free-range egg yolks
2 tbsp lemon juice
Quarter tsp English mustard
A dash of Tabasco
150g salted butter

43

# CILIEGINE MOZZARELLA TREASURE HUNT SALAD

I CALL THIS TREASURE HUNT SALAD BECAUSE AS YOU EAT IT YOU CONTINUALLY UNCOVER LITTLE GEMS OF FLAVOUR AND TEXTURE – YOU NEVER KNOW WHAT MORSEL YOU'RE GOING TO GET NEXT! FEEL FREE TO BE CREATIVE WHEN MAKING THIS SALAD AND ADD WHATEVER TITBITS TAKE YOUR FANCY. THIS SCRUMPTIOUS SALAD OF SURPRISES SHOULD BE BURSTING WITH TEXTURE, FLAVOURS AND COLOURS

## Method

Lightly toast the sourdough bread and cut into cubes.

Carefully dry fry the walnuts and pine kernels.

Then all you need to do is assemble your ingredients and scatter them through a generous helping of salad leaves. I prefer to assemble rather than toss the salad, as you can be a bit more precise and concentrate on the presentation. But in the end it's your salad, so just enjoy it!

Serve in lovely wide, white dishes with a simple dressing of the best-quality organic extra virgin olive oil mixed with a little lemon juice and honey or syrup from the mostarda di frutta.

## Ingredients

300g selection of organic fresh crispy salad leaves – beetroot leaves, rocket and little gem
250g organic buffalo mozzarella ciliegine (small cherry-sized balls)
50g seedless red grapes
50g orange-fleshed melon
Half ripe avocado
25g walnuts
25g pine kernels
1 large slice sourdough bread
1 tbsp mostarda di frutta (an Italian condiment consisting of fruit preserved in a mustard-flavoured syrup)
30ml extra virgin olive oil
2 tbsp freshly squeezed lemon juice
Half tsp honey

# ORGANIC BUFFALO CUSTARD BREAD AND BUTTER PUDDING

## Method

Preheat the oven to 150°C, Gas mark 2.

Whisk the sugar and egg yolks together in a mixing bowl until pale and fluffy.

Using a sharp knife, split half a vanilla pod lengthways and scrape the seeds into a heavy-based saucepan along with the buffalo milk. Gently heat the pan to just below boiling.

Remove from the heat and pour the mixture over the eggs, gradually adding it bit by bit while whisking gently.

Return the mixture to the saucepan and cook gently on a low heat until it coats the back of a spoon, stirring frequently.

To assemble the bread and butter pudding, lay half the buttered bread in an ovenproof dish. Sprinkle over the dried fruits and top with the remaining bread.

Pour over the warm buffalo custard and allow it to sit for 5 minutes.

Cover the pudding with foil and place the dish in a large roasting tin of warm water. Cook in the oven for 30–40 minutes until the pudding is gently set.

Remove from the oven, dust with icing sugar, and glaze under a medium grill to finish. Serve warm.

## Ingredients

Serves 4

For the buffalo custard:
100g caster sugar
6 organic free-range egg yolks
500ml organic buffalo milk
Half a vanilla pod

For the pudding:
12 slices of organic bread, brioche or panettone with the crusts removed, cut into triangles and buttered
50g raisins
50g sultanas
2 tbsp icing sugar

# ORGANIC GAME SCOTCH EGGS

**Method**

Pre-heat the oven to 190°C, Gas mark 5.

Place 4 eggs in a small saucepan with enough water to cover the eggs by 2cm. Place over a high heat. As soon as the water boils, set a timer for 2 minutes. After 2 minutes remove the eggs immediately and plunge into a bowl of iced water to cool.

In a bowl add the minced pork, minced game, thyme leaves and seasoning (add a splash of port or brandy if you wish). Mix thoroughly and form 4 patties with your hands. Chill the mixture in the fridge for 10 minutes.

Once the eggs are cool, carefully remove the shells. Flatten each meat pattie into a round disk and place an egg in the centre. Wrap the meat mixture carefully around each egg to evenly encompass the egg.

Put the flour into a small bowl and season with salt and pepper. In another bowl beat the remaining egg with the milk. Place the breadcrumbs in a third bowl. Then gently roll each meat and egg ball through the flour, gently tap off any excess, then dip into the beaten egg mixture and finally roll through the breadcrumbs. Ensure all sides are evenly coated.

Roll gently in the hands to produce a neat and even finish.

Heat a deep fat fryer with oil deep enough to cover the eggs and heat to 180°C, Gas mark 4. Fry the Scotch eggs for 2–3 minutes until golden brown. Carefully remove from the oil and place on kitchen paper to absorb any excess oil. Place on a baking tray in the pre-heated oven for 10 minutes.

Best served immediately while the yolks are still runny and the Scotch eggs are still warm.

**Ingredients**

Serves 4

5 medium organic free-range eggs
250g minced organic pork belly
250g organic minced game (pheasant, venison, partridge – feathered or furred, whatever is available and in season will work)
Pinch of fresh thyme leaves
Salt and freshly ground black pepper
Dash of port or brandy (optional)
50g plain flour
50ml milk
150g natural dried breadcrumbs
Organic groundnut oil for frying

# BUFFALO BOLOGNAISE WITH BUFFALO MOZZARELLA

**Method**

Sauté the onions and garlic in the olive oil for a few minutes, then add the minced buffalo, continue to fry until the meat is lightly coloured. Add the tomato purée, tinned tomatoes and cherry tomatoes. Stir well and season to taste. Cover and cook over a low heat for 30–40 minutes stirring regularly.

Remove from the heat 1 minute before serving, stir in the drained chopped mozzarella pieces and serve immediately. Perfect served over any organic cooked pasta of your choice.

**Ingredients**
Serves 3–4

500g organic buffalo mince
50ml olive oil
100g finely diced onion
2 cloves of crushed garlic
2 tbsp tomato purée
1 tin of chopped tomatoes
20 organic cherry tomatoes
(washed & halved)
125g ball of buffalo mozzarella
(at room temperature, drained
and cut into 12 pieces)
Salt & pepper to taste

# MERRILEES PARKER
## CELEBRITY CHEF AND TV PERSONALITY

FOR ME, BACK IN THE DAY, FOOD JUST WAS ORGANIC.
I USED TO VISIT MY UNCLE, WHO'S A FARMER IN AYRSHIRE,
AND THAT WAS OBVIOUSLY JUST WHAT WE ATE. WE DIDN'T
THINK ABOUT IT BEING ORGANIC OR NOT. BUT TIMES HAVE
CHANGED AND FOOD JUST DOESN'T TASTE LIKE IT USED TO

" My top organic foods, where it makes a real difference, are
strawberries, chicken, salmon, butter, pork and bread.

I always go back to the taste of food when I was younger, especially
fruit, and I remember these amazing strawberries – we only ate
them in season and they were delicious. Now you see them all the
year round. With meat, in buying organic, you know you're buying
into a high welfare system. Slow-grown pigs are so much better,
and you get much more interesting breeds.

When you go to buy a chicken, it's so important to buy organic –
the difference from the battery end is enormous. People would
be shocked by how cheap chicken is produced. Organic chicken
is the way to go. A real chicken is a treat – you can make it into
three different meals, you don't waste the scraps and you can
make stock and sandwiches.

The idea of us living off the land is unrealistic, but you can take
responsibility for what you buy. Organic salmon is a really good
example, and it is readily available. We can't afford not to eat it.

It might seem odd to highlight organic bread, but it's so important
just how the wheat is grown (though I'm a rye girl myself). I don't
like the idea that there's anything artificial going into the bread I eat,
and that a lot of bread actually has all the goodness taken out, only
to be put back in artificially. I'd buy a good organic loaf that hasn't
been mucked around with. "

Breakfast granola

Bruschette of Cashel Blue with walnut pesto

Crispy chorizo, chilli and palourde clam spaghetti

Curried lamb shanks

Ice cream truffles

# BREAKFAST GRANOLA

**Method**

Preheat the oven to 180°C, Gas mark 4.

Mix together the bran, oats, sesame seeds and walnuts in a non-stick roasting tin.

Drizzle over the oil and maple syrup, tossing until evenly coated.

Bake for 15–20 minutes, stirring halfway through, until crisp and crunchy. Remove from the oven and allow to cool.

Stir the ready-to-eat fruit into the cooled granola and store in an airtight container until required. This will keep very happily for a couple of weeks.

To serve, put a couple of heaped tablespoons of the granola into the bottom of four bowls then mix in the fresh fruit and top with the yogurt mixture.

**Ingredients**

Serves 4

For the granola:
100g organic bran
150g organic jumbo porridge oats
25g sesame seeds
100g walnuts
1 tbsp sunflower oil
5 tbsp maple syrup
100g ready-to-eat mixed fruit, such as Medjool dates and cherries

To serve:
6 tbsp fresh blueberries
1 pear, cored and chopped
1 apple, cored and chopped
2 kiwis, peeled and chopped
1 tub of low-fat organic Greek yogurt

# BRUSCHETTE OF CASHEL BLUE WITH WALNUT PESTO AND WATERCRESS SALAD

**Method**

Heat a griddle pan and a small heavy-based frying pan.

Add the walnuts to the frying pan and toast for about a minute.

Brush the sourdough bread all over with olive oil and season with salt and black pepper. When the griddle pan is smoking hot, toast the bread on both sides, turning at a 90-degree angle to achieve a criss-cross pattern.

Place half of the walnuts in a food processor along with the garlic, lemon juice, zest and plenty of seasoning. Start the blender then slowly add the oil until you have a smooth emulsion.

To serve, cut each slice of bread on the diagonal and place in the centre of each plate. Arrange the Cashel Blue on top. Dress the watercress with the pesto and pile on top, then sprinkle over the remaining toasted walnuts.

**Ingredients**

Serves 2

For the walnut pesto:
50g organic walnuts, roughly chopped
1 clove of garlic
2 tsp lemon juice
1 tsp unwaxed lemon zest
3-4 tbsp extra virgin olive oil

For the Bruschette:
2 slices of organic sourdough bread
100g Cashel Blue or organic well-ripened soft blue cheese, cut into 4 even-sized triangles
A large handful of baby watercress

# CRISPY CHORIZO, CHILLI AND PALOURDE CLAM SPAGHETTI

## Method

Lower the spaghetti into a pan of boiling, salted water, stir once, then cook for 8–10 minutes until al dente.

Meanwhile, heat the light olive oil in a heavy-based saucepan with a tightly fitting lid. Add the chorizo and cook for a couple of minutes until it begins to release its oil and go crispy.

Remove half of the chorizo with a slotted spoon, leaving as much of the chorizo oil in the pan as possible, then drain on kitchen paper.

Add the garlic to the pan and cook for about 20 seconds, stirring constantly.

Turn the heat right up then add the clams along with the sherry. Cover with the lid and leave to cook for 2–3 minutes, shaking the pot occasionally.

When the pasta is cooked, drain it then tip into the pan with the clams and chorizo. Stir in the extra virgin olive oil along with the rocket and plenty of black pepper. Taste before adding any extra salt, as the chorizo and clams are already quite salty.

Serve immediately in warmed deep bowls with the remaining chorizo as garnish.

## Ingredients

Serves 4

350g organic spaghetti
2 tbsp light olive oil
150g organic spicy chorizo sausage, cut into small cubes
2 cloves of garlic, finely chopped
1.5kg Palourde clams
A good dash of Fino sherry
2 tbsp good-quality extra virgin olive oil
2 handfuls of wild rocket

# CURRIED LAMB SHANKS WITH WILD GARLIC RICE

## Method

Preheat the oven to 160°C, Gas mark 3.

Heat 1 tbsp of oil in a large sauté or frying pan with a lid, then add the cardamom pods, cinnamon stick, star anise and cumin seeds. Fry for 1–2 minutes to release the aromas.

Mix the onion, ginger, garlic, chillies and turmeric with 3 tbsp of oil until you have a smooth paste, then add to the pan. Cook for 5–6 minutes until the mixture is fragrant and starting to change colour.

Add the tomatoes, jaggery, chicken stock, coconut cream and a good pinch of sea salt. Stir until well mixed then leave to simmer.

Heat the remaining oil in a large heavy-based frying pan and season the shanks well with salt and pepper. Place in the pan and fry until nicely browned all over.

Add the shanks to the simmering sauce, ensuring they are fully coated.

Place in the oven and cook for 2.5–3 hours, turning at least twice. The meat should be falling off the bone and the sauce lovely and reduced. You may want to skim off some of the fat.

For the rice, heat the ghee in a saucepan with a tight-fitting lid. Add the rice and fry until it turns opaque, then add 200ml of water and a good pinch of salt.

Remove the lid, bring to the boil and allow the rice to absorb all the water. When you see steam holes appearing, put on the lid and turn off the heat. Leave to stand for at least 10 minutes.

Use a food processor to blend the mint and wild garlic with the olive oil until you have a smooth purée.

To serve, stir the wild garlic purée into the rice and pile in the centre of each serving plate. Place a shank on top and finish with plenty of sauce.

## Ingredients

Serves 4

For the shanks:
4 organic English lamb shanks
6 tbsp sunflower oil
6 cardamom pods, lightly crushed
1 cinnamon stick, halved
3 star anise
1 tsp cumin seeds, well toasted then crushed
1 large onion, roughly chopped
1 tbsp chopped fresh ginger
6 cloves of garlic
4 green finger chillies, de-seeded and roughly chopped
2 tsp turmeric
400g chopped tomatoes
2 tsp jaggery (Indian unrefined sugar)
300ml fresh chicken stock
150ml coconut cream

For the rice:
1 tbsp ghee butter
150g basmati rice, rinsed until the water runs clear
25g mint, finely chopped
25g wild garlic, finely chopped
1 tsp olive oil

61

# ICE CREAM TRUFFLES WITH ALMOND AND BISCUIT CRUMB

**Method**

Allow the ice cream to soften enough to scoop easily.

Using a small ice cream scoop or large melon baller, ball the ice cream and place on a metal baking tray. Put the tray in the freezer until the ice cream is frozen solid.

Combine the biscuits with the toasted almonds. Roll each ice cream ball in the dry mixture then dip in the melted chocolate.

Return the truffles to the freezer until ready to serve.

Serve in baby truffle cases or on cocktail sticks.

**Ingredients**

Makes 20–25 truffles

250g good-quality organic vanilla ice cream
6 digestive biscuits, crumbled
50g almonds, toasted and roughly chopped
200g good-quality dark chocolate, melted

# PETER SIDWELL
## CHEF

WHEN I STARTED TRAINING AS A CHEF, NINETEEN YEARS AGO, 'ORGANIC' AS A CONCEPT OR A MOVEMENT WASN'T REALLY AROUND. BUT IT WAS HAPPENING NEVERTHELESS – THEN, AS NOW, PEOPLE WERE GROWING THINGS ON THEIR ALLOTMENTS AND EATING THE FOOD VERY SOON AFTER PICKING OR DIGGING IT UP. I LOVE GROWING MY OWN FOOD AND I'M TEACHING MY YOUNG DAUGHTER ABOUT IT, TOO. IT'S IMPORTANT SHE KNOWS THAT POTATOES COME FROM THE SOIL

Asian beef salad

Roasted tomato and goats' cheese salad

Pork pie with sticky onion chutney

Roasted walnut and rosemary sourdough

Brioche with raspberry and lime jam

"The organic, local, seasonal philosophy really seems to be taking off now – people are more enquiring about the origin of their food, and farmers, as well as chefs, are becoming household names. If you can minimise the length of time between the field and the fork by buying food directly from the farm, then so much the better. You'll be eating food that's in season and picked at the optimal time.

My recipes are all about simplicity, so it's crucial that every ingredient pulls its weight. There's nowhere to hide on my plates, so I make sure to showcase good-quality, organic food that tastes amazing. With a beautiful cut of organic meat, there's no need to add loads of other ingredients, which can reduce the cost of your food bill. If you buy organic food at the right time of year, it doesn't have to break the bank, and with a bit of creativity you can get a good few meals out of an organic free-range chicken.

For me, the organic movement is all about replicating the local, wholesome connection between farmer and food at the retail level. It's about going back to basics and working with, not against, nature to produce unbeatable food. Put simply, organic just makes sense."

# ASIAN BEEF SALAD

**Method**
Heat a griddle pan over a medium heat until smoking hot.

Coat both sides of the steaks with oil and season with plenty of salt and pepper, then cook in the pan for 2–3 minutes on each side.

To make the dressing, grate the ginger and garlic into a mixing bowl and add the rest of the dressing ingredients. Season to taste with salt and pepper.

Cut the steaks into strips and place in the bowl with the dressing.

Chop the salad vegetables into fine matchsticks, as you would for a stir-fry, and arrange on a large flat plate. Add the beef and top with a generous handful of fresh coriander and toasted sesame seeds.

**Ingredients**
Serves 4

2 organic rib-eye steaks
1 tbsp sunflower oil

For the dressing:
1 thumbs' length of fresh ginger
Half a clove of garlic
2 tbsp sesame oil
4 tbsp vegetable oil
2 tbsp dark soy sauce
2 tbsp vinegar
2 tbsp runny honey
1 tsp Chinese five spice

For the salad:
4 carrots
1 red pepper
1 yellow pepper
1 green pepper
1 red onion
4 spring onions
2 handfuls of bean sprouts
Fresh coriander, shredded
Toasted sesame seeds

# ROASTED TOMATO AND GOATS' CHEESE SALAD

**Method**

Preheat the oven to 150°C, Gas mark 2.

Place the sliced tomatoes on a baking tray, cut-side up. Drizzle with vinegar and olive oil and season with thyme, rosemary, salt, pepper and sugar. Roast in the oven for 1 hour.

Tear the ciabatta into small crouton-sized chunks and place in a bowl with the crushed garlic. Add a little olive oil and shake the bowl until the ciabatta is fully coated.

Empty the ciabatta chunks onto a baking tray and cook in the oven for 30 minutes until crisp.

When you are ready to serve, place the slices of goats' cheese on top of the roasted tomatoes and heat under the grill for a few minutes until golden and crisp.

Combine the cheese, tomato, crutons and rocket and coat with a simple dressing of olive oil, vinegar, salt and pepper.

**Ingredients**

Serves 4

8 organic vine tomatoes, halved
Sherry vinegar
Extra virgin olive oil
1 sprig of fresh thyme, chopped
1 sprig of fresh rosemary, chopped
1 tsp sugar
Day-old ciabatta bread
1 clove of garlic, crushed
4 slices of a log of organic goats' cheese
Rocket leaves

# PORK PIE WITH STICKY ONION CHUTNEY

**Method**

To make the pastry, place the flour in a mixing bowl and crumble in the lard. Combine the ingredients until they start to come together. Add a pinch of salt then gradually pour in the water, working with your hands until the dough breaks (it must not be stretchable). Cover and set aside for 1 hour.

Preheat the oven to 190°C, Gas mark 5.

Knead the dough on a floured surface and roll it out to roughly 5mm thick. Divide the dough into two unequal portions. Take a 20cm flan or cake tin with removable base and use the larger portion to line the base and sides. The smaller portion will be used as the pie lid. When lining the tin, make sure there are no holes or tears in the pastry otherwise the jelly will leak out.

To make the filling, mix the pork shoulder, pork fat and bacon, and season with salt and pepper. Place this mixture in the pie case, but don't squash it in. Brush the edges of the dough with water and place the dough lid on top, using a fork to seal the edges together. Brush the top with egg yolk or milk.

Cook in the oven for 1.5 hours until golden brown.

Remove from the oven and turn out from the tin. Leave the pie to cool then place in the refrigerator overnight. The following day, make up the gelatine with the water according to the packet instructions and add any herbs.

Make a hole in the top of the pie and pour in gelatine until the pie is completely filled. Place in the refrigerator overnight. Next day, your pie will be ready to enjoy!

**Ingredients**

For the pastry:
450g flour
225g lard
90ml water
Beaten egg yolks or milk, to glaze

For the pie filling:
450g organic pork shoulder (ask your butcher for the higher meat), finely chopped
55g organic pork fat, finely minced
55g organic bacon, diced

For the jelly:
300ml water
Half sachet powdered gelatine (about 6g)
Your choice of chopped herbs such as parsley, chives or basil

See over for the sticky onion chutney recipe

# STICKY ONION CHUTNEY

**Method**

Melt the butter and oil in a large heavy-based saucepan over a high heat. Tip in the onions and garlic and give them a good stir so they are glossed with butter.

Sprinkle over the sugar, thyme leaves and some salt and pepper. Give the pan a good shake and reduce the heat slightly.

Cook uncovered for 40–50 minutes, stirring occasionally. The onions are ready when all their juices have evaporated, they're really soft and sticky, and they smell of sugar. But they shouldn't be so soft that they break when pressed against the side of the pan with a wooden spoon. The secret to deliciously sweet caramelised onions is slow cooking, so don't rush this part.

Pour in the wine, vinegar and port and simmer, still uncovered, stirring every so often, until the onions are a deep mahogany colour and the liquid has reduced by about two-thirds. When you draw a spoon across the bottom of the pan, it should clear a path that fills rapidly with syrupy juice.

Leave the onions to cool in the pan then scoop into jars and seal. The chutney can be enjoyed straight away, but also keeps in the fridge for up to 3 months.

**Ingredients**

140g butter
4 tbsp olive oil
2kg organic red onions, finely diced
4 cloves of garlic, finely diced
140g golden caster sugar
1 tbsp fresh thyme leaves
75ml red wine
350ml sherry or red wine vinegar
200ml port

# ROASTED WALNUT AND ROSEMARY SOURDOUGH BREAD

## Method

To make the starter dough, mix all the ingredients together in a bowl, cover with a clean tea towel and secure with an elastic band. Leave for 12 hours to prove at room temperature. You will have enough starter dough for 2–3 loaves so use one-third of it for this recipe and store the rest in the fridge for another day. Just remember to add 1 tbsp of flour and 1 tbsp of water to the mix before you use it.

Preheat the oven to 200°C, Gas mark 6.

Place the starter dough in a mixing bowl and add the flours, salt, sugar, yeast and water. Throw in the rosemary and roasted walnuts, too.

Using your hands, mix the ingredients together until they form a dough that comes clean away from the bowl.

Transfer the dough onto a lightly floured work surface and knead the bread for 5 minutes by stretching it away from you, until the dough is smooth and easy to move around.

Place the sourdough back in the mixing bowl, cover and set aside for 30 minutes until it doubles in size. Then knead for a further 2–3 minutes.

Shape into a large round loaf, place on a non-stick baking tray, then leave for a further 30 minutes until it doubles in size again.

Bake in the oven for 20–30 minutes until golden. When you tap the underneath, it should sound hollow.

## Ingredients

Serves 4

For the starter dough:
1 tsp fast action yeast
300g organic strong white bread flour
2 tbsp balsamic vinegar
300ml water
1 tsp sugar

For the bread:
250g starter dough
200g strong white bread flour
50g rye or wholemeal flour
1 tsp salt
1 tsp sugar or honey
1 tsp fast action yeast
125ml warm water
1 handful of organic roasted walnuts
1 tbsp chopped rosemary

# BRIOCHE WITH RASPBERRY AND LIME JAM

## Method

Mix together the yeast, sugar, eggs and milk in a measuring jug.

Place the flour, salt and butter into a mixing bowl then pour in the milky liquid. Using your hands, mix the ingredients together for about 3–4 minutes until it forms a dough that comes clean away from the bowl.

Transfer the dough onto a lightly floured work surface and knead by stretching it away from you, until it is smooth and pliable.

Return the dough to the bowl, cover with clingfilm, and leave to prove in a warm place for 30–40 minutes or until it doubles in size.

Knead the dough on a lightly floured work surface for a further minute.

Divide the dough into 10 equal portions and shape into rolls. Place the rolls on a non-stick baking tray and leave somewhere warm until they double in size again.

Bake in the oven at 200°C, Gas mark 6 for 20–30 minutes or until golden brown on top.

To make the jam, place the raspberries, sugar, lime juice and zest into a pan and mix with a wooden spoon until the sugar is completely dissolved. Cook over a medium heat until the jam boils for 5 minutes.

Leave the jam to cool, then pour into containers. It will keep in the fridge for up to 4 weeks.

## Ingredients

Serves 4

For the brioche:
7g dried yeast
1 tbsp sugar
4 large free-range organic eggs
25ml milk
400g organic strong white flour
Half tsp salt
125g butter

For the jam:
500g organic raspberries
750g preserving sugar
Juice and zest of 1 lime

# GEORGINA DOWNS
## UK PESTICIDES CAMPAIGN FOUNDER

GEORGINA DOWNS IS A NOTABLE CAMPAIGNER, FOUNDING THE UK PESTICIDES CAMPAIGN IN 2001 AND WORKING TIRELESSLY AND CREATIVELY IN THE CAUSE. SHE IS A GREAT ADVOCATE FOR BUYING AND EATING ORGANIC FOOD. GEORGINA'S FAVOURITE ORGANIC MOMENT, ASIDE FROM THE FOOD, IS LYING IN HER LOVELY ORGANIC BEDDING SET

" My favourite organic recipe is roast rack of lamb. But unfortunately we haven't been able to source organic rack of lamb in our area for a few years now, so when you turn to my recipes you'll see a delicious compromise, and it's perfect for an evening meal. "

Roast braised lamb steaks

Organic penne and braised peppers

Tomatoes on toast

Roast chicken

Three pôts de crème

# ROAST ORGANIC BRAISED LAMB STEAKS WITH STEAMED POTATOES AND VEGETABLES

ALL INGREDIENTS INCLUDED IN MY RECIPES WOULD BE ORGANIC WHEREVER POSSIBLE

**Method**

Heat the olive oil in a heavy pan and sear the lamb steaks briefly on each side. Then turn the heat down, cover, and slowly braise for 20–25 minutes.

Wash and peel the potatoes and steam until tender.

Separate the cauliflower into florets and peel and slice the carrots into thin batons. Steam until tender.

Grill the goats' cheese.

Serve the lamb steaks with the goats' cheese, new potatoes and a steaming pile of veg on the side.

**Ingredients**

Serves 4

3 tbsp extra virgin olive oil
4 trimmed organic lamb steaks
350g new potatoes
100g goats' cheese
200g carrots
200g cauliflower

# PENNE WITH BRAISED PEPPERS

I DON'T HAVE THIS MEAL TOO OFTEN AS THE INGREDIENTS ARE QUITE FATTENING, ESPECIALLY HALF A TUB OF ORGANIC GOATS' CHEESE! BUT THIS DELICIOUS AND QUICK RECIPE IS PERFECT FOR AN INDULGENT SUPPER WITH FRIENDS

## Method

Heat some olive oil in a pan and gently fry the peppers until tender.

Meanwhile, boil the penne in water according to the timings on the packet and take off the heat when it's al dente – not too soggy!

Halve the avocado, remove the stone, peel off the skin and roughly chop the flesh.

Drain the pasta, combine it with the peppers and avocado, and crumble over some goats' cheese.

## Ingredients
Serves 4

400g assortment of organic red, green and orange peppers, de-seeded and sliced into strips
4 tbsp extra virgin olive oil
400g penne
1 ripe avocado
150g organic goats' cheese

# TOMATOES ON TOAST

THIS HARDLY QUALIFIES AS A 'RECIPE', BUT REALLY
SHOWCASES HOW GOOD ORGANIC INGREDIENTS CAN
BE. WHEN YOU'VE GOT SOMETHING THIS FRESH AND THIS
GOOD, YOU DON'T NEED TO ELABORATE. I JUST FINISH
WITH A DRIZZLE OF OLIVE OIL, BUT BALSAMIC VINEGAR
ALSO WORKS WELL, ALTHOUGH I TEND NOT TO USE IT

**Method**
Make sure the tomatoes are at room temperature.

Toast the bread and slice the tomatoes.

Heap the tomatoes on the toast, letting the juices soak in.

Drizzle with the oil and vinegar if you like – the perfect
simple breakfast!

**Ingredients**
Serves 2

300g organic large
vine tomatoes
4 slices organic white
bread
Extra virgin olive oil
Balsamic vinegar
(optional)

# ROAST ORGANIC CHICKEN

ANOTHER FAVOURITE ORGANIC MEAL IS ROAST
CHICKEN, ALONG WITH SAGE AND ONION STUFFING,
SEASONAL STEAMED VEGETABLES AND NEW OR
ROASTED POTATOES, DEPENDING ON YOUR
PREFERENCE. I'VE INCLUDED SEASONING IN THE
INGREDIENTS, ALTHOUGH PERSONALLY I DO WITHOUT

**Method**
Preheat the oven to 220°C, Gas mark 7.

To make the stuffing, finely dice the onion and sweat briefly in the
butter. Combine with the chopped sage and breadcrumbs, season
to taste.

Rub the chicken with olive oil, place the stuffing in a baking tray
or in the cavity of the chicken if you wish and place the chicken on
a rack in a roasting tray.

Give the chicken a 20 minute blast at 220°C, Gas mark 7, turn down
the oven to 180°C, Gas mark 4, and cook for 20 minutes per 500g.

Remove from the oven, test carefully that it's cooked through and
leave to rest.

Meanwhile, cook the potatoes to your preference. If roasting, put
them in the oven with the chicken.

Carve the chicken and serve with a portion of the stuffing, potatoes
and steamed seasonal vegetables.

**Ingredients**
Serves 4

1 organic roasting
chicken
50ml olive oil
1 large onion
Bunch of fresh sage
125g breadcrumbs
Knob of butter
500g new or roasting
potatoes
300g seasonal
vegetables
Salt and black
pepper to taste
(optional)

# THREE PÔTS DE CRÈME

**Method**

This recipe contains salt, although personally I do without.

Gently heat the cream with the vanilla pod until bubbles begin to form at the edge, but ensuring the cream does not boil.

Remove from the heat and set aside to infuse.

Melt the chocolates separately in heatproof bowls suspended over saucepans of barely simmering water. (Keep the saucepans of water as you will need them later on.)

Leave the chocolates to cool, and then beat two of the egg yolks into each of the melted chocolates until the mixtures are smooth.

Stir one third of the sugar and salt into each chocolate mixture until completely dissolved.

Remove the vanilla pod from the cream and gently stir one third of the cream into each chocolate mixture until well blended.

Replace the bowls over saucepans of simmering water.

Cook until each mixture coats the back of a spoon, stirring all the time.

Pour each chocolate mixture into your chosen containers and chill for about 2–3 hours or until the mixture has set.

## Ingredients

Serves 4

400ml single cream
1 vanilla pod
25g organic dark chocolate, (minimum 60% cocoa solids, broken into pieces)
25g organic dark orange chocolate, broken into pieces
50g organic white chocolate, broken into pieces
6 large free-range egg yolks
50g sugar
Half level teaspoon salt

# GORDON MCDERMOTT
## EXECUTIVE CHEF,
## WAITROSE COOKERY SCHOOL

ORGANIC MEANS FLAVOUR TO ME. OF COURSE
I CAN CREATE A TASTY DISH USING NON-ORGANIC
INGREDIENTS, BUT THE ORGANIC ALTERNATIVES
HAVE GOT THAT SOMETHING EXTRA THAT'S HARD
TO PUT YOUR FINGER ON. I GUESS YOU JUST CAN'T
BEAT RAW FLAVOUR IN ITS NATURAL FORM

## WILD SALMON, CHARGRILLED ASPARAGUS, SOFT-BOILED EGGS AND SHERRY VINAIGRETTE

**Method**

Boil the eggs for 7–8 minutes, then cool immediately under cold running water. Peel the eggs, cut in half and place on a tray, yolks up.

For the vinaigrette, whisk together all the ingredients and set aside.

Heat a heavy cast-iron griddle pan over a high heat. Brush the salmon on both sides with the melted butter and season with a little salt. Place the fillets in the griddle pan and cook for 4 minutes on each side. Don't be afraid to turn the heat down if the pan's smoking too much.

While the salmon is cooking, brush the asparagus with melted butter. When the salmon is cooked, remove it from the pan and set aside for 2 minutes.

Cook the asparagus in the griddle pan, rolling it gently to ensure it cooks all over. Then remove from the pan and cut in half at an angle.

Divide the asparagus evenly between the 4 plates and lay the salmon fillet on top, with the eggs placed either side of the salmon. Drizzle over the vinaigrette. Serve with freshly boiled Jersey Royals.

**Ingredients**

Serves 4

4 organic free-range eggs
4 x 120g wild salmon fillets
20g unsalted butter, melted
12 asparagus spears, peeled

For the vinaigrette:
1 tsp Dijon mustard
1.5 tbsp sherry vinegar
Half tsp salt
8 tbsp extra virgin olive oil
10g curly parsley, finely chopped

# CAROLE BAMFORD
## DAYLESFORD ORGANIC FOUNDER

AT DAYLESFORD, WE FOLLOW TRADITIONAL FARMING METHODS, WITH ORGANIC AT THE HEART OF ALL WE DO – PRODUCING SEASONAL FOOD AT ITS BEST. THIS IS WHAT ORGANIC MEANS TO ME

# BRAISED SHIN OF BEEF
## FROM THE COOKERY SCHOOL AT DAYLESFORD

**Method**

Remove any large sinews and fat from the shin of beef and cut through the natural seams of the meat.

Place the vegetables in a bowl with the red wine and the beef. Add the thyme, garlic, peppercorns and bay leaf. Place in the refrigerator to marinate overnight. The following day remove the beef from the liquid and allow to dry, then season with salt and pepper.

Preheat the oven to 160°C, Gas mark 2.

Heat a splash of vegetable oil in a heavy-based pan over a high heat then add the beef, cooking until browned all over. Place the beef in a casserole dish and set aside.

Cook the vegetables from the marinade in the same heavy-based pan used for the beef and caramelise over a low heat. Add the tomato purée, the red wine and a sprinkle of flour, and bring to the boil. Add the stock, return to the boil, then skim off any impurities with a small ladle.

Pour the stock mixture over the beef and put a lid on the dish. Place in the oven and cook for 2–3 hours, or longer if necessary. When the beef is cooked, remove the liquid from the pan and pass it through a fine sieve. Then cook the liquid on the stove over a medium heat until it is reduced and thickened. Season to taste and serve with the beef.

**Ingredients**

Serves 4

1 organic shin of beef
2 onions
2 carrots
1 bottle of red wine
Half bunch of thyme
2 cloves of garlic
1 tsp peppercorns
1 bay leaf
1 tbsp tomato purée
3 litres chicken stock
Vegetable oil
Plain flour

93

# January

Bramley apples
Brussel sprouts
Celeriac
Chestnut
Chicory
Date
Kale
Parsnip
Pear
Salsify
Swede

# SEASONAL FRUIT & VEG

WE ALL WANT OUR ORGANICALLY GROWN PRODUCE TO BE FRESH AND FLAVOURSOME, AND THE BEST WAY TO DO THIS IS TO BUY SEASONALLY. HERE'S OUR MONTH-BY-MONTH BREAKDOWN SO THAT YOU KNOW WHAT TO EXPECT FROM YOUR FAVOURITE SUPPLIERS

WINTER

SPRING

SUMMER

# March

Cauliflower
French beans
Jerusalem artichoke
Lemon
Purple sprouting broccoli
Pepper
Rhubarb
Sweet potato

# February

Beetroot
Bramley apples
Cauliflower
Celery
Jerusalem artichoke
Kale
Leek
Rhubarb
Swede
Sweet potato

# April

Cauliflower
Celeriac
New potatoes
Pepper
Sorrel
Spinach
Spring greens
Rhubarb
Watercress

# May

Apricot
Asparagus
Gooseberry
Lamb's lettuce
Pepper
Strawberry
Sorrel
Spinach
Spring greens

# June

Asparagus
Aubergine
Courgette
Fennel
Globe artichokes
Lettuce
Peas
Radish
Raspberry
Sorrel
Spinach
Spring greens
Strawberry
Tomato
Watercress

# December

Bramley apples
Celery
Clementine
Cranberry
Date
Jerusalem artichoke
Pear
Swede
Sweet potato
Turnip

AUTUMN

WINTER

# September

Aubergine
Broad beans
Cabbage
Celery
Damson
Pear
Sweetcorn
Tomato
Watercress
Watermelon

# July

Aubergine
Blackcurrant
Blueberry
Broad beans
Cherry
Courgette
Fennel
Garlic
Peas
Tomato
Watermelon
Watercress

# August

Aubergine
Blackcurrant
Blueberry
Broad beans
Broccoli
Cabbage
Celery
Cherry
Courgette
Fennel
Fig
Sweetcorn
Tomato
Watercress
Watermelon

# October

Aubergine
Bramley apples
Brussel sprouts
Celery
Cranberry
Pear
Swede
Sweet potato
Tomato

# November

Bramley apples
Brussel sprouts
Celery
Clementine
Cranberry
Date
Jerusalem artichoke
Pear
Swede
Sweet potato
Turnip

95

ENJOY WHAT SPRING HAS TO OFFER
WITH THESE DAZZLING SEASONAL MEALS!

# SPRING

# MINI MINTY LAMB KOFTAS

**Method**

Place all the ingredients together in a large bowl.

Mix together with a wooden spoon. Cover with clingfilm and place in the fridge for 30 minutes.

When the mix is cool and you are ready to cook, shape the mix into small kofta-shaped pieces.

To cook, place the kofta under the grill for 10–15 minutes until cooked through and golden in colour.

To make a yummy yogurt dressing perfect for dipping, mix a few dessert spoonfuls of organic Greek yogurt with some chopped coriander, mint and some finely diced cucumber.

Serve with pieces of warmed naan bread and a few wedges of cucumber.

**Ingredients**

450g organic lean minced lamb
1 large carrot, grated
3 spring onions, finely sliced
1 clove of garlic, crushed
50g fresh breadcrumbs
2 tsp tomato paste
1 dsp fresh mint, roughly chopped
1 dsp fresh coriander, roughly chopped

# TROUT AND MASCARPONE PARCELS

**Method**

Preheat the oven to 180°C, Gas mark 4.

Roll out the puff pastry into four 15cm squares and lay them out in front of you.

Scoop 1 tbsp of the Mascarpone cream into the middle of each square of pastry.

Top with some of the smoked trout, the fennel seeds and a dash of fresh tarragon.

Season with a little salt, freshly ground black pepper and a squeeze of lemon juice.

Beat an egg, then use a pastry brush to brush the liquid over the edges of the pastry.

To close up the parcels, bring two opposite corners together and pinch them in the middle. Repeat with the remaining two corners so that your parcel is sealed.

When all the parcels are sealed, brush the outside of the pastries with the remaining egg wash then place them on a baking tray lined with non-stick parchment.

Bake in the oven until golden-brown.

These taste equally delicious when served either hot or cold, and for a perfect cocktail party hors d'oeuvre simply make tiny ones.

**Ingredients**

Serves 4

375g organic
puff pastry
250g organic
mascarpone cream
4 organic smoked
trout fillets
2 tbsp fresh tarragon,
or 1 tbsp dried
1 lemon
2 free-range eggs,
beaten
1 tbsp fennel seeds

# SLOW-ROASTED LAMB MARINATED IN SAFFRON-INFUSED YOGURT

**Method**

Make a few deep cuts on the surface of the lamb.

Place the garlic cloves, ginger and lemon juice in a food processor and blend to form a paste.

Place the saffron strands or turmeric in a small bowl with the sugar and salt and pour over 1 tbsp hot water. Let it soak for 5 minutes.

Mix together the garlic paste, saffron mixture, chilli powder, yogurt and 2 tbsp of the oil. Pour over the lamb and rub into the cuts.

Marinate for 4–6 hours or overnight.

Preheat the oven to 170°C, Gas mark 3.

Heat the remaining oil in a casserole dish large enough to fit the lamb. Add the sliced onions and whole spices and sauté until softened but not brown.

Add the leg of lamb then seal the dish, using either foil or a lid. Place in the oven.

After 90 minutes, remove the foil or lid and baste the lamb.

Cook for a further 30 minutes without a covering until the lamb is golden-brown, tender and completely cooked through.

Allow the lamb to rest for 10 minutes before carving. Spoon over the onions and pan juices to serve.

**Ingredients**

1 small leg of organic British lamb, about 1.2–1.5kg in weight
2 cloves of garlic, crushed
2cm piece of root ginger, grated
Juice of 1 lemon
1 tbsp saffron strands or turmeric
Pinch of sugar
Pinch of salt
Half tsp chilli powder
125g organic Greek-style yogurt
4 tbsp olive oil
2 onions, sliced
2 star anise
1 cinnamon stick, broken in half

# ROASTED TOMATO AND BASIL PESTO PASTA

## Method

Slice the tomatoes in half and place them onto a baking tray cut side facing up.

Drizzle with vinegar, a little oil and season with salt, pepper, chopped thyme and rosemary.

Finally sprinkle the sugar evenly over the tomatoes, this will bring out the natural sweetness of the tomatoes and make them really yummy.

Roast in the oven for 1 hour at 150°C, Gas mark 2.

Put the basil, parmesan, garlic and pine nuts into a food processor and season well.

Whizz together and with the motor still running, pour the oil in until the pesto thickens, finish with a squeeze of lemon juice to taste.

Store in a clean jar in the fridge covered with a slick of oil to prevent it drying out.

Cook the pasta in salted boiling water for 9–12 minutes.

When the pasta is cooked, drain in a colander and return to the same pan you cooked the pasta in.

Simply add in a few tablespoons of pesto, followed by the roasted tomatoes and mix together.

To serve scatter a few extra pine nuts over the top followed by some shaved Parmesan cheese.

## Ingredients

Serves 4

12 organic vine tomatoes
1 tsp of sugar
1 sprig of thyme
1 sprig of rosemary
375g organic pasta
50g basil
30g pine nuts, toasted
30g Parmesan cheese, freshly grated
1 clove garlic, peeled and crushed
85ml olive oil
Half a lemon
Salt and freshly ground black pepper

# PASTA PRIMAVERA

**Method**
Cook the pasta according to the packet instructions.

Drain and keep warm.

Heat the oil in a deep frying pan or wok, and add the mixed vegetables. Toss over a high heat for 1 minute.

Add the pasta and the pesto sauce. Turn for 30 seconds. Remove from the heat, add the yogurt, season to taste with salt and pepper and serve immediately.

**Ingredients**
Serves 4

50g fresh pasta spirals
or quills
1 tbsp olive oil
Handful mixed organic
vegetables such as
mange tout, baby sweet
corn, sugar-snap peas,
carrot sticks, red and
green peppers and
bean sprouts
1 tbsp pesto
2 tbsp natural yogurt
Salt and freshly ground black
pepper

# CINNAMON-SPICED YOGURT PANCAKES WITH MIXED BERRY COMPOTE

## Method

To make the compote, simply place the berries and compote in a small pan and gently simmer for 5–10 minutes until the berries soften. This can be served hot or cold with the pancakes.

To make the pancakes, mix together the egg yolks, yogurt and vanilla extract in a small bowl.

Sift the flour, baking powder, cinnamon and sugar in a separate bowl, then mix in the yogurt mixture to form a batter.

Beat the egg whites until stiff. Fold into the batter gently.

Heat a little olive oil in a frying pan and add spoonfuls of the batter. Cook in batches for 2–3 minutes on each side until golden-brown. Serve warm with the compote drizzled on top.

**Quick tip:** You can save time by preparing the batter the night before, but don't whisk up the egg whites until you're ready to make the pancakes. You can also prepare the compote in advance and then warm it up as the pancakes are cooking.

For blueberry pancakes, simply add a few fresh blueberries to the pancake mixture with the egg whites.

## Ingredients

For the Compote:
1 pot of fruit compote
250g mixed organic berries, fresh or frozen

For the Pancakes:
2 free-range eggs, separated
450g organic vanilla yogurt
A few drops of vanilla extract
100g self-raising wholemeal flour
100g plain flour
2 tsp baking powder
1 tsp ground cinnamon
1 tbsp caster sugar

# PARADISE PIE

**Method**

The Banoffee pie has had a makeover. This recipe combines that famously delicious mix of chewy chocolate base, sticky toffee sauce and bananas with a tropical coconut cream topping.

Preheat the oven to 180°C, Gas mark 4.

Mix together the biscuits, cereal and butter until thoroughly combined.

Press the mixture into a 20cm tart tin with a removable base, making sure the layer of mixture is flat and even.

Bake the biscuit base for 10 minutes until slightly darker in colour and firm to touch. Leave to cool.

Layer the bananas over the base and spread the condensed milk on top.

Whip the cream, yogurt and icing sugar together and gently spoon soft peaks over the sauce.

Lightly dust with cocoa powder for decoration.

Try serving with an extra drizzle of cream – scrumptious.

**Ingredients**

Serves 4

150g digestive biscuits, crushed
70g chocolate granola and nuts
30g unsalted butter, melted
2 organic bananas, sliced
397g condensed milk
180g double cream
100g organic Greek-style coconut yogurt
1 tbsp icing sugar
1 tsp organic cocoa powder, for dusting

# HOT CROSS BUN AND APRICOT BUTTER PUDDING

**Method**

A wonderful Easter alternative to the traditional bread and butter pudding. The sweet and spicy buns and apricots make a superb combination together with the creamy yogurt and milk. A delicious family pudding.

Preheat the oven to 180°C, Gas mark 4.

Slice the buns vertically into thick slices and butter one side of each slice.

Grease an ovenproof dish with a little butter and arrange the bread slices on the base, overlapping slightly. Scatter over the apricots.

Place the eggs, milk, yogurt and sugar in a bowl and whisk to mix thoroughly. Pour the mixture over the bread and apricots.

Place the dish in a large roasting tin. Fill the tin halfway up with boiling water. Bake for 30–40 minutes until the pudding is just set.

Serve with Greek yogurt or crème fraiche.

**Ingredients**

Serves 4–6

4 organic hot cross buns
50g butter
125g dried apricots, chopped
3 free-range eggs, beaten
275ml organic whole milk
200g organic Greek-style yogurt
50g soft brown sugar

# YOGURT AND OAT COOKIES

## Method

Preheat the oven to 195°C, Gas mark 5.

Line or grease a baking tray.

In a bowl, cream together the butter and sugars until light and fluffy.

Stir in the yogurt and vanilla extract and mix well.

Add the flour and bicarbonate of soda and continue to mix until all the flour is incorporated.

Add the spelt flakes.

Drop tablespoons of the mixture onto the prepared sheet and bake for 8–10 minutes until golden brown on the edges.

Leave to cool slightly before removing onto a wire cooling rack.

Try adding some chocolate chips for extra indulgence!

## Ingredients

Makes 18 biscuits

80g organic unsalted butter or margarine
100g caster sugar
110g light soft brown sugar
80g organic natural yogurt
A drop of vanilla extract
180g plain flour
Half tsp bicarbonate of soda
130g organic toasted spelt flakes

AL FRESCO DINING, SALADS GALORE AND
PERFECTLY RIPE FRUIT – BRING ON THE SUMMER!

# SUMMER

# SPICY PRAWNS WITH APPLE AND MINT YOGURT CHUTNEY

**Method**

Mix together the prawns and the rest of the ingredients, except the fresh coriander leaves. Marinate the prawns in a covered dish in the refrigerator, for a minimum of 2 hours or overnight.

To cook, thread the prawns onto wooden or metal skewers and place under the grill for about 5 minutes until golden-brown in colour. Turn regularly to ensure an even colour all over.

Sprinkle over the fresh coriander leaves and serve with the apple and mint chutney.

To make the chutney, place the mustard seeds in a non-stick pan and sauté until they sizzle and pop.

Whisk together the rest of the chutney ingredients and then stir in the mustard seeds.

Cover and chill until required. This will keep in the refrigerator for up to 2 days.

**Quick tip:** If using wooden skewers, soak them for 30 minutes in cold water first to prevent them burning during cooking.

**Ingredients**
Serves 12

For the Prawns:
450g large raw prawns, peeled and deveined
100g organic low fat natural yogurt
2 tbsp fresh lemon juice
1 clove of garlic, crushed
1 tsp paprika
1 tsp garam masala
Half tsp ground cumin
Half tsp ground coriander
1 tbsp fresh coriander leaves, chopped

For the Chutney:
1 tsp black mustard seed
300g organic fat free natural yogurt
Half tsp salt
1 tsp root ginger, finely chopped
2 tbsp mint, finely chopped
1 eating apple, cored, peeled and finely chopped
Fresh lemon juice, to taste

# KING PRAWN THAI-STYLE SALAD

**Method**

To make the dressing, use a pestle and mortar to pound the clove of garlic and half the red chilli into a smooth paste. If you do not have a pestle and mortar, you can use a bowl and a wooden spoon.

Combine the rest of the dressing ingredients, only tasting the dressing when all the ingredients have been added. Adjust the quantities to taste and, as with all salad dressings, add the salty ingredient in moderation – in this case the Thai fish sauce.

To serve, place all the salad ingredients in a bowl and cover with the dressing, tossing the salad a couple of times so it is well combined.

Garnish with fresh coriander and the julienne slices of chilli.

**Ingredients**

For the dressing:
1 clove of garlic
1 red chilli – chop half to use in the dressing, and slice the other half julienne style for garnishing
2 tbsp organic Greek-style coconut yogurt
Juice of half a lime
1-2 tsp Thai fish sauce

The salad itself:
1 serving of cooked king prawns
1 good handful of organic bean sprouts
4 thick slices of organic cucumber cut at an angle and in half
3 spring onions, chopped at an angle
1 small handful of fresh coriander

# BABA GANOUSH OR AUBERGINE DIP

**Method**
Preheat your grill or barbecue.

Prick the aubergines with a fork and grill for about 20 minutes, turning occasionally, until the skins are blackened and the flesh is soft.

Remove from the grill and place in a colander, allowing the excess liquid to drain off. Leave to cool.

When cool, remove the skin and head, transfer the flesh to a food processor and blend until you have a purée.

Add the garlic, lemon, chilli, parsley and yogurt, and blend again.

Season with cumin, salt and black pepper, garnish with a sprinkle of parsley, and serve straight away.

This dish is delicious served with warm pitta bread, and perfect as an accompaniment to grilled lamb dishes.

**Ingredients**
2 large organic aubergines
2 cloves of garlic, finely chopped
Juice of half a lemon
1 red chilli, de-seeded and chopped
2 tbsp of fresh flat-leaf parsley, finely chopped, plus a sprinkling more for garnishing
5 tbsp organic Greek-style natural yogurt
Good pinch of ground cumin

# CANNELLONI STUFFED WITH SPINACH AND ALMONDS

**Method**

Preheat the oven to 150°C, Gas mark 2.

Cook the cannelloni in boiling water until al dente. If using ready-to-use pasta, ignore this step.

Place 1 tsp of butter in a large pan, melt and add the spinach. Cook fast, shaking the pan, until the spinach is half its bulk. This should take less than 3 minutes. If using frozen spinach, ignore this step.

Place the spinach in a bowl and add the almonds, the remaining butter, the crème fraiche, Gruyere cheese, and season with salt and pepper. Mix well.

Drain the cannelloni sheets. Lay a portion of the spinach mixture on a sheet and roll into a cylinder. Or, stuff the ready-made tube with 1 tbsp of the spinach mixture. Continue filling and rolling, tucking in the ends so they are underneath.

Lightly grease a large, shallow ovenproof dish with butter and lay the cannelloni in side by side so they fit snugly. Pour over the cream, sprinkle with Parmesan and bake for 20 minutes until the cannelloni is hot all the way through and the cheese has melted.

Sprinkle with toasted flaked almonds and serve piping hot.

**Ingredients**

Serves 4–6

12–16 sheets or tubes of cannelloni
900g organic leaf spinach or large pack frozen spinach
2 tbsp butter
225g ground almonds
2 tbsp crème fraiche or Greek-style natural yogurt
Half cup of Gruyere cheese, grated
225ml organic single cream
Half cup of Parmesan cheese, grated
Sprinkle of toasted flaked almonds

# NIÇOISE SALAD

**Method**

To make the dressing, whisk together the olive oil, red wine vinegar, parsley, chives and garlic, and season with salt and pepper.

Place the tuna in a shallow dish and pour over half the dressing. Marinate for 1–2 hours in a covered dish in the refrigerator, occasionally turning in the marinade to ensure even coverage.

Heat a ridged griddle pan on the hob or a hot barbecue for 5 minutes.

Remove the tuna from the marinade and cook the steaks for 2–3 minutes on each side, depending on how rare you like your fish.

Place all the salad ingredients in a bowl and add the tuna.

Drizzle over the remaining dressing then finish by adding the eggs, olives and basil leaves.

**Ingredients**

Serves 4

For the dressing:
7 tbsp extra virgin olive oil
3 tbsp aged red wine vinegar
2 tbsp freshly chopped parsley
2 tbsp freshly snipped chives
2 cloves of garlic, peeled and finely chopped

For the salad:
450g responsibly sourced fresh tuna or 4 x 175g tuna steaks, each 2.5cm thick.
8 organic new potatoes, cooked and quartered
4 plum tomatoes, roughly chopped
115g extra-fine green beans, topped and tailed, cooked, and drained
1 red onion, finely sliced
4 organic free-range eggs, cooked for 6 minutes in boiling water from room temperature and then sliced in half
16 pitted black olives in brine
8 basil leaves, shredded

# CHOCOLATE AND CHERRY BROWNIES

**Method**

Preheat the oven to 180°C, Gas mark 4.

Take a baking or roasting tin measuring 35 x 25cm and at least 6cm deep and line it with greaseproof paper or baking parchment.

Melt the butter and chocolate together in a heatproof bowl suspended over a saucepan of barely simmering water.

Beat the eggs, sugar and vanilla extract together in a bowl until the mixture is thick and creamy and coats the back of a spoon.

Once the butter and the chocolate have melted, remove from the heat and beat in the egg mixture.

Sift the flour and salt into the mixture, and continue to beat until smooth.

Stir in the dried cherries.

Pour the mixture evenly into the roasting tin and bake in the oven for 20–25 minutes or until the whole of the top has formed a light-brown crust that has started to crack. This giant brownie should not wobble, but should remain gooey on the inside.

Leave to cool for about 20 minutes before cutting into large squares while still in the pan. The greaseproof paper or baking parchment should peel off easily.

**Hint:** Try adding nuts or other dried fruits as an alternative to the cherries, or even make plain chocolate brownies without any extras at all – they're equally tasty!

**Ingredients**

Makes 28 brownies:

300g unsalted butter
300g organic dark chocolate (minimum 60% cocoa solids), broken into pieces
5 large free-range eggs
450g granulated sugar
1 tbsp vanilla extract
200g plain flour
1 tsp salt
250g dried cherries

# CHOCOLATE AND AMARETTO PANNA COTTA

**Method**

In need of a chocolate fix? Then try this sensational dessert –
a delicious and indulgent variation on the classic Italian dish.
The mingling of rich, dark chocolate with creamy yogurt, spiked
with Amaretto, is simply irresistible. This dish is also perfect for
entertaining as it can be made well in advance.

Brush 6 x 150ml pudding basins or ramekin dishes with a little
sunflower oil.

Place 4 tbsp of the milk in a bowl and sprinkle over the powdered
gelatine. Leave to stand for 5 minutes.

Combine the remaining milk, sugar and chocolate and melt over
a low heat, stirring frequently.

Heat the gelatine and milk mixture over a low heat until dissolved,
but do not allow it to boil. Then pour the gelatine mixture into the
chocolate milk and whisk to combine.

Leave the mixture to cool to room temperature, then whisk in the
Amaretto and yogurt.

Pour the mixture into the pudding basins. Cover and leave to set
in the refrigerator for at least 6 hours or overnight.

To remove from the mould, slide a knife around the edges then
invert onto a plate and shake once, firmly.

Decorate the tops of the panna cottas with curls of dark chocolate
and accompany with fresh berries.

**Ingredients**

Serves 6

225ml organic
whole milk
1 tbsp powdered
gelatine or
vegetarian equivalent
4 tbsp caster sugar
170g organic plain
chocolate, chopped
4 tbsp Amaretto
325g organic natural
yogurt

# BERRY CRUNCH LAYER

**Method**

For a healthy summer dessert, try this delicious and easy-to-assemble crunchy fruit fool. This also makes a perfect light breakfast or healthy snack – packed full of a range of nuts, seeds and berries, it provides plenty of the essential omega fatty acids, protein, vitamins and minerals needed to keep you feeling energised throughout the day.

Lightly toast the nuts and desiccated coconut in a non-stick pan over a medium heat until golden-brown.

Once cool, combine with the pumpkin seeds and use the pulse setting of a food processor or blender to coarsely chop the mixture, being careful not to process it too heavily. Stir in the flaxseed.

Gently combine the berries and the yogurt, spoon into glasses, and top with the nut and seed mixture. Serve immediately.

**Storage:** The nut and seed topping will keep in an airtight container for up to 2–3 days but is best assembled and eaten immediately.

**Ingredients**

Serves 3–4

For the topping:
30g desiccated coconut
3 tbsp almonds
3 tbsp hazelnuts
3 tbsp pumpkin seeds
1 tbsp ground flaxseed

For the berry and yogurt layer:
200g organic fresh blueberries or mixed berries
200g organic fat free blueberry yogurt

133

# ELDERFLOWER CORDIAL

**Method**

Boil the water, dissolve the sugar, and stir in the citric acid.

Slice the lemons thinly and add to the syrupy water. Add the elderflower heads. Leave covered in a cool place to steep for 48 hours.

Strain through muslin and put into sterilised bottles.

It's a lovely refreshing drink just with water or add sparkling water for an elderflower spritzer.

**Ingredients**

For every 2 pints of water:
2 organic lemons
75g citric acid
(available from chemists)
20 elderflower heads
4lbs organic granulated sugar

THERE ARE SOME UNMISSABLE TREATS
IN THE AUTUMN LARDER – TUCK IN!

# AUTUMN

# ROASTED ORGANIC CARROT SALAD

**Method**

Preheat the oven to 200°C, Gas mark 6.

Combine the carrots, almonds and garlic in a mixing bowl. Drizzle with the olive oil then season to taste with salt and pepper. Spread out on an ungreased baking sheet.

Bake the carrots in the oven for about 30 minutes until soft with brown edges. Remove and cool to room temperature.

Once cool, return the carrots to the mixing bowl and drizzle with honey and vinegar, tossing them until fully coated.

Add the cranberries and blue cheese and toss again until evenly mixed.

Combine with the rocket and serve immediately.

**Ingredients**

Serves 6

900g organic carrots, peeled and thinly sliced at a diagonal angle
55g slivered almonds
2 cloves of garlic, minced
60ml extra virgin olive oil
5ml honey
15ml cider vinegar
40g dried cranberries
100g Danish blue cheese, crumbled
40g rocket

# ROASTED CARROT AND HUMMUS DIP

**Method**

This dish makes a tasty change to traditional hummus and is perfect for a light lunch, snack or autumn appetiser. Not to mention the fact that the high vegetable content of this recipe puts you well on your way to eating your 5-a-day.

Preheat the oven to 220°C, Gas mark 7.

Place the carrots in a small roasting tin, add the garlic, cumin and 1 tbsp of the olive oil, and toss to mix.

Place the garlic under the carrots and roast for 15–20 minutes or until the carrots are tender and lightly charred.

Add the chickpeas to the roasting tin and stir well to coat them with the cooking juices.

Remove the skin from the garlic and discard.

Transfer the ingredients to a food processor, add the remaining oil and lemon juice, then use the pulse setting to blend to a creamy pureé. Season to taste with salt and pepper.

Transfer to a bowl and serve with the vegetable crudités.

**Ingredients**
Serves 4

For the hummus:
350g organic carrots, washed, trimmed and cut into 2cm chunks
3 cloves of garlic, unpeeled
2 tsp cumin seeds
2 tbsp olive oil
1 tin of organic chickpeas in water, drained
Juice of 1 lemon

For the crudités:
1 carrot, peeled and cut into batons
1 green pepper, cut into batons
10 cherry tomatoes
10 mushrooms

# LAMB MOUSSAKA

**Method**
Preheat the oven to 190°C, Gas mark 5.

Fry the lamb in a frying pan without any oil until the fat runs
off, then drain and set aside.

Use 1 tbsp of the olive oil to fry the onion until soft but not
browned.

Add the lamb, chopped tomatoes and tomato purée, season to
taste with salt and pepper, and cook on a low heat until hot through.

Saturate the aubergine slices in the remaining oil, adding more oil
if necessary and fry gently.

When the aubergine slices are cooked until slightly brown, remove
them from the heat and blot with kitchen paper to absorb some
of the excess oil.

Place the mince mixture in an ovenproof dish, cover with the
aubergine slices and top with yogurt.

Cook in the oven for about 30–40 minutes until the top is bubbling
and slightly golden. Garnish with parsley and serve piping hot.

For an ideal accompaniment to this dish, try a crisp salad or
a hearty portion of steamed spinach and broccoli.

**Ingredients**
Serves 4

1kg minced organic
lamb
1 onion, chopped
6 tbsp olive oil
2 large tins of
chopped tomatoes
with herbs
4 tbsp tomato purée
3 organic aubergines,
thinly sliced
200g organic Greek-
style natural yogurt
Small handful of fresh
parsley, chopped

# PARMESAN ROAST CHICKEN WITH ROASTED CHERRY TOMATOES

**Method**

Preheat the oven to 180°C, Gas mark 4.

Place the chicken breasts on a non-stick baking tray and top them with the grated cheese. Season with the chopped thyme and salt and pepper.

Lay the vines of tomatoes around the chicken, then mix together the oil, vinegar and sugar to form a dressing.

Pour the dressing over the tomatoes then cook the whole lot in the oven for 20–25 minutes until the chicken is cooked through and the Parmesan cheese is golden.

Garnish with the basil leaves and serve.

**Ingredients**

Serves 4

4 organic chicken breasts, skinless and boneless
150g Parmesan cheese, grated
1 tbsp fresh thyme, chopped
4 large vines of organic cherry vine tomatoes
8–10 tbsp extra virgin olive oil
4 tbsp balsamic vinegar
Half tsp granulated sugar
Small handful of freshly torn basil leaves

# TOFU AND
# SHIITAKE STIR-FRY

**Method**

Drain the tofu and use kitchen paper to gently squeeze out any excess water.

Cut the tofu into cubes and coat lightly with the cornflour. Fry the tofu in the sesame oil in a pan until golden-brown.

Meanwhile, cook the ramen noodles as instructed on the packet, then drain and put to one side.

Remove the stalks from the shiitake mushrooms and add them, the red pepper and the spring onions to the tofu, adding extra oil if necessary.

After frying for approximately 1 minute, add the soy sauce to taste.

Combine the stir-fry with the ramen noodles and serve.

**Ingredients**

Serves 4

1 block of organic tofu
25g cornflour
2 tbsp sesame oil
4 x 88g brown rice ramen noodles
25g shiitake mushrooms, rehydrated 1 hour before cooking
Shoyu or Tamari soy sauce
1 red pepper, sliced into strips
2 spring onions, sliced into strips

# FRUIT COBBLER

## Method

The mouth-watering fruit cobbler lies somewhere between a crumble and a pie. With tart and juicy garden fruits and berries covered in a sweet and crunchy topping, it's a perfect comfort pudding for those blustery autumn evenings.

Preheat oven to 200°C, Gas mark 6.

Place the berry mix in an ovenproof dish.

In a small bowl, mix half the caster sugar with the mixed spice and cornflour. Sprinkle this over the fruit and gently combine.

Take the sifted flour, butter and the remainder of the sugar and use the pulse setting of a food processor to blend them together until the mixture resembles breadcrumbs.

Add the yogurt and blend again to form a soft and sticky dough.

Spoon this mixture over the fruit in scattered clumps, leaving some gaps for the cobble effect. Sprinkle the top with muesli and sugar.

Bake for 40 minutes or until the fruit is tender and the top is pale golden.

Delicious served warm with cream or ice-cream.

For a variation, try adding some sliced Bramley apple or pear to the fruit mix.

## Ingredients

Serves 4–6

300g organic berry mix, either fresh or frozen
200g golden caster sugar, plus extra for sprinkling
Half tsp ground mixed spice
3 tbsp cornflour
175g self-raising flour, sifted
75g unsalted butter, cubed
125g organic low fat natural yogurt
25g fruit and nut muesli

# PLUM AND CARDAMOM BRULÉE

**Method**

Heat the oven to 150°C, Gas mark 2.

Cut the plums into small chunks and place in the bottom of 6 ramekin dishes.

Place the cream and the cardamom pods in a pan and heat to just below boiling. Then remove from the heat and leave to infuse for 30 minutes.

Whisk the egg yolks with the caster sugar and add the yogurt.

Whisk the yogurt mixture into the cream.

Strain the cream to remove the cardamom, then pour into the ramekins over the plums.

Place the ramekins in a small roasting tin and pour hot water into the tin until the ramekins are half immersed.

Bake for 20–30 minutes until the mixtures are just setting. Allow to cool, then chill for 2–3 hours or overnight.

Just before serving, sprinkle some caster sugar about 2mm thick over the surface of the ramekins. Brown under a very hot grill or melt with a blowtorch until the surface is golden and caramelised.

**Ingredients**

Serves 6

4 organic plums
300ml double cream
6 cardamom pods, crushed
6 free-range egg yolks
1 tbsp caster sugar, plus a few more spoonfuls for sprinkling on top
250ml organic Greek yogurt

# TOFFEE APPLE YOGURT CAKE

**Method**

Preheat the oven to 180°C, Gas mark 4.

Using an electric mixer, beat the butter and sugar together until light and fluffy.

Gradually beat in the eggs, adding a teaspoon of flour if the mixture begins to curdle.

Sieve and then fold in the flour and cinnamon, followed by the yogurt and apple.

Divide the mixture between two greased and lined 17.5cm sandwich tins and cook for 20–25 minutes until golden and springy to the touch.

Turn the cakes out of their tins and cool on a wire rack.

To make the icing, beat the butter until fluffy then gradually add the icing sugar, stirring until smooth. Add the yogurt and mix well, being careful not to over-beat.

Sandwich the cakes together with the icing, and sprinkle the extra caster sugar over the top.

**Tip:** If toffee yogurt's not your thing, try using organic Greek-style yogurt with honey or natural yogurt with vanilla.

**Ingredients**

Serves 6

For the cake:
175g unsalted butter, softened slightly
175g golden caster sugar, plus a little extra for sprinkling on top
3 large free-range eggs, beaten
200g self-raising flour
Half tsp ground cinnamon
45ml organic toffee yogurt
1 Cox's apple, cored and diced

Icing:
75g butter
175g icing sugar
2 tbsp organic toffee yogurt

# MICAH'S TRUFFLES

## Method
Place the chocolate in a large bowl. Bring the cream to the boil and pour it over the chocolate. Stir gently until the chocolate has melted, trying not to create bubbles. Leave to cool for 2 minutes, then add the butter in two stages and stir in gently. Once the butter is incorporated, the ganache should be smooth and glossy with no oil slick on the surface. Set the truffle mixture in the fridge for a minimum of 3 hours or overnight.

Remove the ganache from the fridge about 15 minutes before you want to make the truffles, depending on room temperature.

Put the cocoa into a bowl. Ensure your hands are cold and dry, then dust them with cocoa. Take spoonfuls of the ganache mixture (use a teaspoon or a tablespoon, depending on how large you like your truffles) and roll the mixture into a ball in your cocoa-dusted hands.

Drop each shaped truffle into the bowl of cocoa, turn it around and then toss it between your palms to remove any excess powder. The truffles can then be returned to the fridge and kept for up to 2 days as long as they are stored in an airtight container.

## Ingredients
Makes 36 truffles

275g organic dark chocolate, (minimum 60 per cent cocoa solids, broken into pieces)
250ml organic double cream
50g unsalted butter, at room temperature
50g cocoa powder

STRONG AND HEARTY THEY MAY BE, BUT THERE'S NO REASON FOR WINTER MEALS TO BE GREY AND STODGY. READ ON!

# WINTER

# CHESHIRE CHEESE MELT WITH APPLE AND RED ONION RELISH

**Method**

Stuck for good ideas for a tasty snack? Then try a slice of this oh-so-tasty cheese on toast with a twist. The apple and red onion relish is easy to make, and you could double the quantities to keep some extra in the fridge for up to three days. Then you can make more of this delicious bite at a moment's notice.

Preheat the grill to high.

Heat the olive oil in a frying pan and add the butter and onion. Cook over a medium-low heat, stirring often, for a few minutes.

Add the apple slices and cook until softened.

Sprinkle in the sugar and cook until the onion and apple turn a rich golden-brown.

Remove from the heat and stir in a few drops of balsamic vinegar.

Toast the slices of farmhouse loaf or ciabatta bread on one side only under the grill.

Then remove from the grill and heap the onion and apple mixture onto the untoasted sides.

Top with the Cheshire cheese and a sprig or two of rosemary or thyme.

Season with salt and freshly ground black pepper.

Toast under the grill for a few moments until the cheese starts to melt and bubble. Serve at once.

**Ingredients**
Serves 2

1 tbsp olive oil
Small knob of butter
1 onion, red or white, thinly sliced
1 red apple, cored and thinly sliced
Half tsp caster sugar
A few drops of balsamic vinegar (optional)
2 thick slices of crusty farmhouse loaf or ciabatta bread
100g organic Cheshire cheese, cut into slices (don't worry if they crumble)
Fresh sprigs of rosemary or thyme

# CHEDDAR CHEESE AND CORN MUFFINS

**Method**

Preheat the oven to 200°C, Gas mark 6.

Mix together the self-raising flour, baking powder, salt, sugar, grated cheese and sweetcorn.

Melt the butter in a pan then mix in the mustard, yogurt, milk, egg and chives.

Pour this mixture into the flour and mix briefly to combine.

Spoon a small amount of the batter into lightly greased muffin tins. Place a piece of cheese in the centre of each muffin then top with the remaining batter.

Place in the oven and bake for 20–25 minutes until golden, then turn out and place on a wire rack.

Serve warm.

**Tip:** Using wholemeal flour will provide you with additional fibre and nutrients and can help to sustain energy levels for longer.

For an even stronger flavour, why not try lightly frying a couple of rashers of organic streaky bacon until golden, then chopping them up and adding them to the muffin mixture. Or you could try substituting the sweetcorn for some chopped organic tomato.

**Ingredients**

Makes 12 approx

300g organic self-raising flour, either white or wholemeal
2 tsp baking powder
Pinch of salt
1 tsp sugar
75g mature organic Cheddar cheese, grated
75g canned sweetcorn, drained
60g butter
1 tsp English mustard
150g organic Greek-style yogurt
175ml whole milk
1 free-range egg
1 tbsp fresh chives, chopped
50g mature organic Cheddar cheese, cut into 12 small chunks

# CREAMY CHESTNUT AND PARSNIP SOUP

**Method**

Preheat the oven to 220°C, Gas mark 7.

Peel the parsnips. Cut into rounds – larger ones for the skinny end of the parsnip and thinner ones as you work your way to the top.

Tumble them into a roasting dish and top with 1 tbsp rapeseed oil and the crushed peppercorns.

Roast in the oven for 30 minutes until tender but not browned.

Score the chestnuts with a little cross. Place in a baking dish and roast in the oven for 20 minutes.

Shell the roasted chestnuts, cover with a cloth to keep them warm and moist, and set aside.

Heat 1 tsp rapeseed oil in a pan then sauté the onion, garlic and apple until tender but not browned. Pour over the stock then add the parsnips and their juices, and the shelled chestnuts. Simmer for 10 minutes.

Mix the milk and cream together.

Take the pan off the heat and blend it with a hand blender, slowly adding in the milk/cream until the mixture is a purée. For a really silky-smooth texture, pass the soup through a fine-mesh sieve.

**Ingredients**

Serves 4

5 medium-sized organic parsnips
1 tbsp plus 1 tsp rapeseed oil
2 black peppercorns, crushed
25 chestnuts
1 small onion, peeled and finely diced
2 cloves of garlic, peeled
1 small apple, peeled and finely diced
750ml chicken or vegetable stock
100ml whole milk
50ml pouring cream

# KIPPERS AND POACHED EGGS

**Method**

Preheat the oven to 180°C, Gas mark 4.

Tear 4 pieces of baking parchment or foil into 50cm lengths. Drizzle a little olive oil onto the middle of the paper and place the kippers on top.

Season with the butter, slices of lemon and black pepper then splash with a little water.

Fold the kippers into sealed parcels, place on a baking tray, and cook for 15 minutes. Then turn off the oven and leave the fish to sit while you poach the eggs and put on the toast.

To poach the eggs, bring a large pan of water to a simmer, add the vinegar, and gently break the eggs into the pan. Lift out with a slotted spoon when done and drain on kitchen paper.

Serve the kippers and poached eggs on buttered toast, topped with freshly ground black pepper.

**Ingredients**

Serves 4

4 kippers
50g butter
1 lemon
8 organic free-range eggs
30ml white wine vinegar
4 doorstop-sized slices of organic bread

# THAI GREEN CURRY

**Method**

This trusty favourite, jam-packed full with flavour, is quick and easy to prepare. Feel free to follow your nose with this one and throw in a few handfuls of cooked prawns, organic chicken or vegetables to bulk up this scrumptious and winter-warming dish.

Cook the noodles according to the packet's instructions, then rinse under cold water.

Make the curry paste by placing the spring onions, chillies, lime zest, lime leaves, lemon grass and garlic in a food processor and blending until you have a smooth paste.

Heat the groundnut oil in a wok and pour in the curry paste, cooking gently for 3–4 minutes, stirring occasionally.

Pour in the coconut milk and cook for a further 2 minutes.

Add the noodles and heat through.

Serve with the pistachio nuts sprinkled on top.

**Ingredients**

Serves 4

225g organic rice noodles
4 spring onions
2–3 green chillies, de-seeded
Zest of 4 limes
6 Kaffir lime leaves
2 small lemon grass stalks
2 cloves of garlic
3 tbsp groundnut oil
1 tin of organic coconut milk
150g pistachio nuts, lightly toasted

# TURKEY BURGERS WITH APPLE AND CRANBERRY SAUCE

## Method

To make the sauce, place the sliced apple in a saucepan with 1 tbsp cold water and cook over a low heat for 12–15 minutes, stirring occasionally, until the apples have softened.

Add the dried cranberries then remove from the heat and blend with a hand blender until almost smooth. Set aside.

To make the burgers, mix the turkey mince in a bowl with the spring onions and black pepper. Add the egg, the cornflour and mix with your hands.

Form the meat into golf-ball sized patties and flatten slightly with your palm.

Brush the burgers with olive oil, then grill or pan-fry on a medium heat until both sides are browned and the inside of the burger is no longer pink.

Cut the roll in half down the middle then stuff with a handful of rocket, a turkey burger and finish with a dollop of sauce.

Unfortunately, these burgers aren't suitable for freezing – although after you taste these, it's unlikely there'll be any left over to freeze anyway!

## Ingredients

Makes 20 mini burgers

For the sauce:
200g organic apples, cored, peeled and sliced
50g dried cranberries

For the burgers:
500g organic turkey mince
4 organic spring onions, finely chopped
Half tsp freshly ground black pepper
1 medium free-range egg
2 tsp cornflour (optional)
1 tbsp olive oil
100g rocket
10 mini wholemeal pitta breads, or rolls of your choice

# PORK AND MUSHROOM CASSEROLE

**Method**

Preheat the oven to 180°C, Gas mark 4.

Pour 150ml boiling water over the dried porcini mushrooms and leave them to soak for 15 minutes. Then strain through a fine sieve and reserve the liquid as it passes through.

Heat the oil in a large casserole dish and fry the pork fillet for 5-6 minutes until lightly browned.

Add the onion, garlic, chestnut mushrooms and Porcini mushrooms. Cook in a pan for 1–2 minutes until the onion starts to soften.

Add the wine, cream and half the sage and bring to the boil.

Cover the casserole with a lid and place in the oven. Cook for 40–45 minutes or until the pork is completely cooked through with no pink juices. If the casserole starts to dry out before the pork is cooked, add the reserved mushroom water.

Season with freshly ground black pepper then sprinkle over the remaining sage to serve.

This comforting winter dish requires little effort to create, but tastes divine, making it perfect for cosy family suppers or get-togethers with friends. Serve with rice and leafy greens to soak up the delicious creamy sauce.

**Ingredients**

Serves 4

20g dried Porcini mushrooms
2 tbsp olive oil
450g organic pork fillet, cut into large chunks
1 onion, chopped
2 cloves of garlic, crushed
200g organic chestnut mushrooms, quartered
2 tbsp fresh sage, chopped
150ml Marsala wine
250g double cream or crème fraiche

# TARRAGON-BAKED CHICKEN AND CARROTS

**Method**

Preheat the oven to 190°C, Gas mark 5.

Scrub the carrots clean and trim off the tops, then place them in a large roasting tin.

Add the oil, garlic, lemon juice, a third of the tarragon and plenty of salt and freshly ground black pepper, then toss well to mix.

Mix the butter with the lemon zest, remaining tarragon and some more black pepper.

Divide the butter into four portions, then use your fingers to push each quarter under the skin of a chicken breast fillet.

Lay the chicken breasts skin-side up on top of the carrots and bake for 25–30 minutes until the carrots are lightly charred and the chicken is golden and tender.

Serve with green vegetables and new potatoes.

**Ingredients**

Serves 4

400g organic carrots with tops
2 tbsp olive oil
1 clove of garlic, chopped
Zest and juice of 1 lemon
20g fresh tarragon, trimmed and chopped
50g butter, softened
4 organic chicken breast fillets with skins on
Salt and freshly ground black pepper

# ALMOND COOKIES WITH CHERRY YOGURT ICING

**Method**

Preheat the oven to 190°C, Gas mark 5.

Sieve the flour into a bowl.

Cut the butter into small chunks and add to the flour, rubbing in until the mixture resembles breadcrumbs.

Stir in the sugar, almonds and half the yogurt.

Grease two baking trays and place spoonfuls of the mixture onto the trays, pressing down to form thick cookie shapes.

Bake in the oven for 20–25 minutes until golden-brown, then turn out to cool on a wire rack.

Sieve the icing sugar and mix in the remaining yogurt, adding more if necessary, to make a runny icing. Ice the biscuits using a teaspoon or palette knife and leave to set.

For Valentine's Day cookies, roll out the dough and cut into heart shapes, bake as before and make the icing slightly thicker by adding an extra 35–50g icing sugar.

**Ingredients**

Makes around 20 cookies

175g organic plain flour
100g butter, at room temperature
50g caster sugar
4 tbsp organic cherry yogurt
50g blanched almonds, roughly chopped
100g icing sugar

# MEAT CUTS

DO YOU KNOW YOUR SIRLOIN FROM YOUR SILVERSIDE, YOUR FLANK FROM YOUR FILLET? HERE'S A QUICK WHAT'S WHAT TO HELP YOU CHOOSE YOUR CUT OF BEEF, PORK OR LAMB TO SUIT YOUR MOOD AND OCCASION

ALL THESE CUTS CAN BE EASILY FOUND IN YOUR LOCAL BUTCHER OR SUPERMARKET AND IF YOU'RE STUCK, JUST ASK FOR ADVICE!

## SPECIAL OCCASIONS

For special occasions, splash out on a leg of pork for roasting, or a rack of lamb. And you can't get more British than a roast beef sirloin on the bone for carving. You could also serve the ultimate in luxury, a fillet of beef with a béarnaise sauce and French fries or use it in the classic dish, beef wellington.

## FAMILY FEASTS

For a frugal feast, pot roast a beef brisket or shin, or a lamb scrag. Cuts from the forequarters of the animal are usually cheaper, as these muscles work the hardest and require slower methods of cooking if you have the time. Hindquarter cuts are tender, and are better if you are in a hurry as they are easily roasted or fried – minute steaks, taken from the thick flank, are the cheapest in this category. Pork shoulder and belly are on the cheaper end of the scale (that's why they're used in sausages!), but out of these two, you'll get more flavour for your money with the shoulder.

## QUICK MEALS

For a quick and healthy mid-week meal, go for a pork tenderloin or a thin beef fillet steak. Lamb in general tends to be a pretty fatty meat, but opt for a leg steak if you're after a lighter option. If you're strapped for time, pan-fry some lamb chump chops, or grill a rump steak and slice up for a salad.

# CONVERSIONS

## Liquid measurements

| | |
|---|---|
| 5ml | 1 teaspoon (tsp) |
| 10ml | 1 dessertspoon (dsp) |
| 15ml | 1 tablespoon (tbsp) or $1/2$ fl oz |
| 30ml | 1 fl oz |
| 60ml | 2 fl oz |
| 75ml | $2 1/2$ fl oz |
| 100ml | $3 1/2$ fl oz |
| 150ml | 5 fl oz ($1/4$ pt) |
| 300ml | $1/2$ pt |
| 450ml | $3/4$ pt |
| 600ml | 1 pt (20 fl oz) |
| 1 litre | $1 3/4$ pt |

## Oven temperatures

| °C | °F | Gas Mark | Oven |
|---|---|---|---|
| 140 | 275 | 1 | Cool |
| 150 | 300 | 2 | |
| 170 | 325 | 3 | Moderate |
| 180 | 350 | 4 | |
| 190 | 375 | 5 | Moderately Hot |
| 200 | 400 | 6 | |
| 220 | 425 | 7 | Hot |
| 230 | 450 | 8 | |
| 240 | 475 | 9 | Very Hot |

## Weights

| | |
|---|---|
| 15g | $1/2$ oz |
| 25g | 1oz |
| 50g | 2oz |
| 75g | 3oz |
| 110g | 4oz ($1/4$lb) |
| 150g | 5oz |
| 175g | 6oz |
| 200g | 7oz |
| 225g | 8oz ($1/2$lb) |
| 250g | 9oz |
| 275g | 10oz |
| 300g | 11oz |
| 350g | 12oz ($3/4$lb) |
| 375g | 13oz |
| 400g | 14oz |
| 425g | 15oz |
| 450g | 16oz (1lb) |
| 500g | 1lb 2oz |
| 675g | 22oz ($1 1/2$lb) |
| 1kg | 2.2lb |

All conversions are approximate

# THANK YOU

## FIRST, A VERY BIG THANK YOU TO ALL THE CONTRIBUTORS TO THE BOOK. THANKS FOR YOUR TIME AND YOUR MOUTH-WATERING RECIPES WHICH ARE HELPING TO SHOW THAT ORGANIC FOOD AND DRINK IS FOR EVERYONE

Also a very big thank you to all those organic companies and organisations that have funded this recipe book and the Why I Love Organic campaign. Together we can achieve so much.

Those who produced the book also need a big hearty thanks – the team at Haygarth: Tara, Katie, Nicola and Hatti; RMC Brainwave; my wonderfully supportive colleagues at Sustain: the alliance for better food and farming; and the Organic Trade Board.

Finally, a thank you to you for buying and enjoying this book and seeing that organic food is simply great tasting, natural food!

Catherine Fookes
CAMPAIGN MANAGER
WHY I LOVE ORGANIC

## GET INVOLVED

We hope you've been inspired – not to mention well fed! – by the recipes in this book, and also by the personal stories of people who love organic food. Maybe you'd like to hear more?

There are many ways you can get involved in the Why I Love Organic campaign – visit our website at: **www.whyiloveorganic.co.uk**

Here you can tell us your reasons for loving organic, joining famous names such as Sara Cox, Sarah Beeney and Tom Aikens. There's lots more info about everyday organic food, including loads more recipe ideas. Maybe you've got your own favourite organic recipe? You can add yours here too.

You can also sign up to receive more information on organic via our website, and join us on Facebook and Twitter. We'd love to hear from you, so keep in touch with us at: **www.whyiloveorganic.co.uk**

# INDEX